A COMMENTARY ON
THE EPISTLE
TO THE PHILIPPIANS

F. W. BEARE

Professor of New Testament Studies
Trinity College, Toronto

HARPER & BROTHERS, PUBLISHERS
New York

UXORI DILECTAE
INTER MULIERES BENEDICTAE,
QUAE ETIAM SEDENS SECUS PEDES DOMINI
AUDIT VERBUM ILLIUS,
HUNC LIBRUM
LAETO ANIMO
DEDICAVI

Fortitudo et decor indumentum ejus,
et lex clementiae in lingua ejus.
Confidit in ea cor viri sui.

A COMMENTARY ON THE EPISTLE TO THE PHILIPPIANS

Copyright © 1959 by Francis Wright Beare

Printed in the United States of America

Library of Congress catalog card number: 59-7145

HARPER'S NEW TESTAMENT ❧ COMMENTARIES ❧

edited by HENRY CHADWICK

This distinguished series is achieving in our generation what the classic Bible commentaries did in theirs. It summarizes the knowledge of years of scholarly study and interpretation and relates this understanding organically to the contemporary situation in the church.

Each commentary is by a top authority in England and America (see back flap); gives new, clear and authoritative translations; illuminates the historical background; stresses the lasting and contemporary relevance of the writings; considers fully the questions of doctrine; utilizes the best features of past commentaries, combined with the most up-to-date critical thought; provides the basic materials for sermons.

"The launching of the Harper series of New Testament commentaries was undoubtedly one of the most important events in Biblical scholarship in 1958."
> —REGINALD H. FULLER, *Professor of New Testament, Seabury-Western Theological Seminary*

"If the rest of this series is equal to its first volumes, British and American readers will have available a group of commentaries unsurpassed in any language. The authors face almost all the relevant issues and combine critical and theological insights in such a way as to create the best commentaries available in English."
> —ROBERT M. GRANT, *The Federated Theological Faculty, University of Chicago*

"This new series of commentaries has made an auspicious beginning . . . we await with eagerness the appearance of the remaining volumes which promise to combine the results of highly technical scholarship with penetrating insights into the doctrinal import of the New Testament."
> —BRUCE M. METZGER, *Princeton Theological Seminary*

"The individual scholars both in the commentaries published and the projected volumes of the series are solid scholars of theological sensitivity as well as academic depth."
> —FRANK M. CROSS, JR., *Harvard Divinity School*

HARPER'S
NEW TESTAMENT COMMENTARIES
GENERAL EDITOR: HENRY CHADWICK, D.D.

———————————

THE EPISTLE TO THE PHILIPPIANS

PREFACE

To spend six months in the study of the Epistle of St. Paul the Apostle to the Philippians is a most rewarding and at the same time a shattering experience. No one can make a sustained effort to understand this epistle without a constant deepening of his conviction of the truth and reality of the Christian faith; or without a growing sense of his own deficiencies and half-heartedness as a follower of Christ Jesus the Lord. The glowing intensity of the Apostle's devotion makes our own seem flickering and fitful, and altogether unworthy of the joy that is set before us, the prize of the high calling of God in Christ Jesus. Yet the very words which reveal to us the extent of our own failure stir us to the depths and encourage us to join in imitating Paul and those who like him forget the things that are behind and strain eagerly towards the things that lie ahead, speeding on in the hope that they may win, as they have been won by Christ Jesus.

Like many before me, I have found some things hard to understand in the writings of our beloved brother Paul; and I can only hope in the Lord that I have not wrested them to my own destruction, or to the misguiding of any of my readers. At least I will make bold to say that nothing is set down here to promote anything other than the truth of the gospel. 'Seeing we have this ministry, as we have received mercy, we faint not; but have renounced the hidden things of dishonesty, not walking in craftiness, nor handling the word of God deceitfully; but by manifestation of the truth commending ourselves to every man's conscience in the sight of God' (2 Cor. iv. 1-2).

I am most grateful to my colleague, Professor E. R. Fair-weather, for his kindness in preparing for me the splendid article on 'The "Kenotic" Christology', which is printed at the end of this volume as an Appended Note. It will perhaps serve as an indication of the possibilities that lie open for fruitful collaboration between New Testament scholars and

v

specialists in philosophical and dogmatic theology. The constant opportunities that I have for discussing with him all manner of questions which involve the inter-relation of our two disciplines are to me one of the many delights of working in Trinity College.

I could wish that something of the same kind might have been done for me in the matter of the significance of this epistle for the history of Ascetic Theology. No commentary known to me has undertaken to offer an interpretation of this aspect of the Apostle's teaching, nor has it been possible for me to undertake such a study myself—it lies outside the realms of my competence. It would be most helpful to have a dissertation on the influence of Philippians on the ascetic discipline of the Church. More broadly, I am convinced that all of us in the churches of the West would gain much by inquiring into the interpretation of St. Paul in the tradition of the Eastern Orthodox; it would help us to escape from the trammels of controversy which for four hundred years have ranged us for or against Luther. *Vixerunt fortes ante Agamemnona.*

This commentary is designed primarily for the use of readers who do not know Greek. In our time, many theological students must be included in this category. Chiefly for their benefit, I have given extensive bibliographies, in which I have noticed books and articles in French and German as well as in English; and I have even ventured to cite a few sentences from Desiderius Erasmus in Latin. It is hoped that neither these nor the occasional Greek words which I have felt it necessary to introduce will interfere with the enjoyment of the commentary by readers who have no knowledge of the classical languages.

Trinity College,   F. W. BEARE
   Toronto, Canada
July 1958.

CONTENTS

ABBREVIATIONS

The commentaries are cited by the name of the author, with the page(s) of the edition listed in the bibliography.

ATR   *Anglican Theological Review.*

AV   Authorized Version.

BKW   Bible Key Words (see under *ThWB*).

DB Supp   *Dictionnaire de la Bible*, ed. F. G. Vigouroux ; *Supplément*, ed. L. Pirot, A. Robert and H. Cazelles (in progress, vols. i to v complete ; Fasc. XXX [first of vol. vi] published in 1957 ; Abdeh-Mythes). Paris : Letouzey & Ané.

ET   *Expository Times.*

HDB   Hastings' *Dictionary of the Bible*, 5 vols., Edinburgh : T. & T. Clark ; New York : Scribners, 1898-1904.

HTR   *Harvard Theological Review.*

JBL   *Journal of Biblical Literature.*

JTS   *Journal of Theological Studies* (n.s. = New Series).

Lxx   The Greek Old Testament in the Septuagint Version.

NTS   *New Testament Studies.*

RB   *Revue Biblique.*

RHPR   *Revue de l'Histoire et de la Philosophie Religieuse.*

RSR   *Recherches de Science Religieuse.*

RSV   American Revised Standard Version of the Bible, London and New York : Nelson, 1946.

RThP   *Revue de Théologie et de Philosophie*

ThWB   *Theologisches Wörterbuch zum Neuen Testament*, ed. G. Kittel, vols. i to v complete, vol. vi in process of publication. Stuttgart : Kohlhammer, from 1933.

Eight articles from the *Wörterbuch* are now available in English (1958), as follows :
Bible Key Words (*BKW*), translated and edited by J. R. Coates and H. P. Kingdon. London : A. & C. Black ; New York : Harper, 1949-1957.

    I. *Love*, by G. Quell and E. Stauffer.

    II. *The Church*, by K. L. Schmidt.

    III. *Sin*, by G. Quell, G. Bertram, G. Stählin, and W. Grundmann.

    IV. *Righteousness*, by G. Quell and G. Schrenk.

    V. *Gnosis*, by R. Bultmann.

    VI. *Apostleship*, by K. H. Rengstorf.

    VII. *Basileia*, by K. L. Schmidt.

    VIII. *Lord*, by W. Foerster and G. Quell.

EPISTLE TO THE PHILIPPIANS

INTRODUCTION

1. AUTHENTICITY AND INTEGRITY OF THE EPISTLE

THERE is abundant external evidence for the authenticity of Philippians. It was undoubtedly included in the first collection of the Pauline epistles, which must have been made before the end of the first century; it is not only cited, but mentioned as a letter of St. Paul's, by Polycarp, Bishop of Smyrna (not later than A.D. 170; probably as early as 135); and it appears in all lists of canonical writings among the epistles of St. Paul. The question of its authenticity was raised for the first time in 1845 by F. C. Baur (*Paulus der Apostel Jesu Christi*); he and some other scholars of his school denied it to St. Paul, on grounds that are no longer regarded as serious by anyone. The style, diction, and spirit are characteristically Pauline, and it is now universally accepted as an authentic composition of the great Apostle of the Gentiles.

The question of integrity is another matter. It is widely held, even if general agreement cannot be claimed, that our Philippians is a composite of portions of two or more letters.

(1) The great hymn of ii. 6-11 is regarded by nearly all commentators as a composition framed prior to and independently of the epistle. To some of them, it seems at least open to hold that Paul himself was the composer (M. Dibelius, E. F. Scott, and others). More and more, however, are persuaded that it is not the work of Paul himself, but that he has made use of a Christian hymn which was familiar to his readers. Most of those who take this position also think of it as a 'pre-Pauline' hymn; it is suggested in the commentary that this is an unwarranted conclusion. Even if it be granted that the hymn is not of Paul's own composing, it does not by any means follow that it reflects a pre-Pauline Christology. It is at least equally possible that it is the expression of a Christology formed under the influence of Paul, within his circle, by a gifted Gentile

convert who ventured to sing of Christ in language borrowed from the praises of one of those 'divine Heroes' whom he had formerly honoured with his devotions.

So long as it is held that Paul himself incorporated the hymn into the epistle, the question of its authorship does not affect the integrity of the document. A few scholars, however, regard the hymn as post-Pauline, and treat it accordingly as an interpolation, introduced by an editor of the second or third generation. Thus Alfred Loisy spoke of it as 'a short poem of Christian gnosis', which was probably added 'about the beginning of the second century' (*The Birth of the Christian Religion*, trans. L. P. Jacks [London: George Allen & Unwin, 1948], p. 26 and note on p. 364). This hypothesis is incidental to the radical reconstruction of the development of Christian thought in the first and second centuries as Loisy pictured it, which required him to deny important sections of all the Pauline epistles to St. Paul. There are insuperable difficulties in the way of accepting any such hypothesis of large-scale interpolations. For one thing, there would be no point in interpolating the epistles before they were collected and published; if the interpolations were introduced at the time of publication, one would expect them to show a much greater degree of homogeneity (among themselves and against the original 'Paul'); and once they were published and in circulation, how could such interpolations be introduced and impose themselves on the church, without leaving any trace in the tradition of the text? It is quite impossible to imagine any circumstances under which this hymn could have been introduced into an epistle already in circulation.

(2) It is suggested by Professor J. H. Michael and others that the little section concerning the sending of Timothy (ii. 19-24) contains such incongruities with the epistle as a whole as to raise the question whether it is not a fragment of another epistle: 'a brief Pauline note . . . written to correspondents whose identity can no longer be determined, at a time when the Apostle chanced to be surrounded by persons who had not drunk deeply of the spirit of Christ' (Michael, *Commentary*, p. 112). The rather bitter words, 'They are all looking after their own affairs, not the things of Christ Jesus' (ii. 21) are

somewhat surprising, so soon after he has paid tribute to 'some' at least of the local Christians who are 'daring more and more boldly to preach the word without fear . . . moved by love, knowing that I am set for the defence of the gospel' (i. 14, 16). However, we believe that the interpretation offered in the notes makes it possible to accept the passage as an integral part of the epistle.

(3) Much more weight must be attached to the observation that there is a very abrupt break at iii. 1: 'a break so harsh as to defy explanation' (Goodspeed). It can hardly be explained as merely an instance of the spontaneity which is to be expected in an informal personal letter (Philippians is neither so personal nor so informal as all that!). The simplest hypothesis is probably that which is proposed by Professor Goodspeed himself (*Introduction to the New Testament* [Chicago: University of Chicago Press, 1937], pp. 90-96). He suggests that Philippians as it has come down to us is a composite work, containing two letters, written at an interval of about a year, the later coming first. The earlier of the two, consisting of iii. 2-iv. 20, was written soon after Epaphroditus arrived from Philippi with the gifts of the church; the later, consisting of i. 1-iii. 1 and iv. 20-23, was written as Epaphroditus was on the point of returning to Philippi after a long and serious illness. A similar view of the structure was proposed by Loisy (*op. cit.* p. 27; Loisy, however, allows for some substantial interpolations), and by several earlier writers, from the late seventeenth century on (*see* M. Goguel, *Introduction au Nouveau Testament*, iv, 1 [Paris: Leroux, 1925], pp. 404 ff.).

Others have attempted to solve the problem in another way. Recognizing the abruptness of the break, they think not of two letters somewhat awkwardly joined, but of a single letter with a long interpolation, beginning with iii. 2 (or with 1b, which is hard to deal with in any case). Within this group, there is further disagreement over the extent of the interpolated material. Some would carry the interpolation as far as iv. 3, taking the letter proper to resume with the repeated 'farewell' (or 're-joice') of iv. 4. The majority would carry it to iv. 1. Michael has attempted to show that it ends with iii. 19; he feels that the phrase: 'For we are a colony of heaven' (Moffatt's rendering)

3

follows unnaturally after vv. 16-19, but fits admirably after iii. 1a (rendered 'rejoice in the Lord'). Others have gone so far as to suggest that almost the whole of chapters iii and iv consists of a succession of disconnected fragments, written at different times and places; and that we are to look on Philippians 'as an editorial organization of parts of several letters which Paul wrote. . . . Probably the letter in its final form was put together by the Christian leader who collected Paul's letters and published them as a corpus' (*New Testament Life and Literature* by D. W. Riddle and H. H. Hutson [Chicago: University of Chicago Press, 1946], pp. 123-125).

It is suggested in this commentary that the interpolation extends from iii. 2 to iv. 1, and that the difficult phrases of iii. 1b form a half-apologetic introduction to the appeal to Evodia and Syntyche to work in harmony; the appeal for unity addressed to the whole church (ii. 2-3) is now pointed directly to the two women. The Apostle might well feel reluctant to get to the point of naming the parties to the disputes in the church which so much disturbed him; but it hardly seems likely that he would put off the difficult moment by indulging in a slashing attack on Jewish propagandists and Christian libertines.

(4) It is further suggested that the little section iv. 10-20 is a fragment of another letter, which was sent to thank the Philippians for their gift soon after the arrival of Epaphroditus. It is inconceivable that the Apostle should never have acknowledged its receipt during the months that must have passed before Epaphroditus recovered from his dangerous illness and was ready to travel home again; especially as there had been an exchange of communications between Paul and the Philippians during the interval (ii. 26).

The epistle appears, on the view here put forward, to be composed of three elements, as follows: (i) a letter of thanks, perhaps complete except for its salutation, acknowledging the gift which had been brought to the Apostle in his prison by Epaphroditus (iv. 10-20); (ii) a letter despatched with Epaphroditus on his return to Philippi, intended partly to make the Philippians think more highly of him than ever, and partly to dissolve tendencies towards self-assertiveness and partisanship in the Philippian church, which seem to have grown around

4

the rivalry of two women (i. 1-iii. 1; iv. 2-9, 21-23); and (iii) a long interpolation in the second letter, warning the readers against Jewish propaganda and against shameful self-indulgence (iii. 2-iv. 1).

Finally, it should be said that many of the best scholars in the world have remained fully convinced that the epistle is a unity—a single letter, composed wholly on the one occasion, without any interpolations. It will suffice to mention C. H. Dodd, M. Dibelius, E. Haupt, E. Lohmeyer, and E. F. Scott, among critics of the twentieth century who have maintained this view.

2. The Destination of the Epistle. Philippi and the Philippian Church

The church of Philippi was the first of St. Paul's foundations in Macedonia. The story of its beginnings is told in Acts xvi. 9-40. Paul and his companions, Silas and Timothy, after leaving Derbe and Lystra, had passed rapidly through 'the Phrygian and Galatian country', quite evidently seeking a new field of labour, in keeping with Paul's eagerness 'to preach the gospel, not where Christ has been named' (Rom. xv. 20), but where no one had yet heard of him. Prevented from undertaking work in Asia (the Roman province of that name, which consisted of the western coastal regions of the peninsula, facing upon the Aegean), they made an attempt to turn north into Bithynia, the wealthy and populous province which lay along the south shore of the Black Sea; but again they found it impossible to carry out this plan. The nature of the hindrances is not indicated; the apostles were content to see in them indications that the Spirit of Jesus, to whom they looked for guidance, was forbidding them to evangelize these provinces at this time. They went on as far as Alexandria Troas, the last port of Asia, near the entrance of the Hellespont (Dardanelles). This would seem to indicate that Paul was already envisaging a journey into the western provinces of the Empire with the gospel of Christ. At all events, they were guided in that direction by a vision which appeared to Paul in the night: 'there stood a man of Macedonia who besought him, "Come over into Macedonia and help us"' (v. 9). They took this as clear evidence of the divine leading, and sailed forthwith for Neapolis, the port of Philippi and the eastern terminus of the great military road known as the Egnatian Way, the chief avenue of communication between Rome and the East.

The city of Philippi lay less than ten miles inland from Neapolis. It took its name from Philip II of Macedon, the father of Alexander the Great, who laid it out on the site of a little settlement known in earlier times as The Springs (*Krenides*). Until that time, it had been an obscure Thracian village; but a few years earlier (360 B.C.), an Athenian exile named Callistratus had brought in some Greek families from Thasos, and Philip now fortified the place and gave it a garrison of Macedonians (357 B.C.). It was to be a military strong point in the Thracian country which he had subdued, and at the same time it would guard the gold mines near by, which yielded him an annual revenue of as much as a thousand talents (the equivalent of many millions of our depreciated pounds). After the battle of Pydna (168 B.C.), it was included in the first of the four districts into which Macedon was divided for Roman administration (*Macedonia Prima*), to be incorporated into the Province of Macedonia in 146 B.C. Almost nothing is known of its history during the next century; but in 42 B.C. it became world-famous as the scene of the great battle in which the Caesarian forces of Antony and Octavian defeated the Republican generals Brutus and Cassius, the assassins of Julius Caesar—the victory which paved the way for the creation of the Roman Empire under the sovereignty of Octavian, the future Augustus. Antony at once settled a number of his disbanded veterans in Philippi, and it was made a 'colony' (in Roman terms, a military settlement, with exceptional civic privileges). In 30 B.C., Octavian, not long after his victory at Actium, where he defeated the combined forces of Antony and Cleopatra to emerge as undisputed ruler of the Roman world, introduced a second contingent of Latin-speaking settlers, consisting mainly of families expelled from certain regions of Italy which he was expropriating for the mass settlements of veterans who would form a dependable reserve for him nearer home. He now dignified the city with the honourable name of Colonia Augusta Julia Philippensis.

At the middle of the first century A.D., when Paul and his companions arrived, the city still reflected this Latin and military cast. Its chief magistrates were called 'generals' (*strategoi*; not Praetors, but *duumviri iure dicundo* was the Latin term), who were accompanied by lictors with axe and rods; like Rome itself, it had quaestors, aediles, and flamens of the Imperial cult; the people thought of themselves as 'Romans' (Acts xvi. 21), and Latin was the official language. But the Latin families, though probably the most numerous, were by this time largely influenced by the Graeco-Oriental environment in which they had now been living for nearly a hundred years. The indigenous Thracian element was still of some importance, and probably continued to recruit itself from the countryside; and the Greek (Thasian) and Macedonian families, which had settled there in the fourth century and afterwards, still formed an important part of the population. Besides all this, Philippi was the first station on the Egnatian Way; it was the gateway between Asia and the West; and it included among its inhabitants traders and artisans from Anatolia, Syria, and perhaps even Egypt. It is significant that Paul's first convert was a woman of Thyatira, a merchant of purples trading in the products of a city of Asia.

In religion, the Philippi of St. Paul's day exhibited a remarkable variety of divinities and cults; the syncretism of the age is found here in one of its most ample expressions. Archaeological investigation, incomplete and partial though it has been, has yielded names and symbols of native Thracian deities, of the gods of Greece and Rome, and of the great divinities of the Orient—importations from Anatolia, Syria, and Egypt; with different deities often receiving a cult at a common shrine. In the city itself, the monuments of the imperial cult were undoubtedly the most conspicuous; inscriptions make mention of flamens and priests (*sacerdotes*) of Divus ('the deified') Julius, Divus Augustus, Divus Claudius; and there are monuments of Victoria Augusta (the divine spirit that gives Augustus the victory), of the Augustan Peace (*Quies Augusta*), and of the Fortune and the Genius of the colony. The Greek gods, who had certainly had their altars and temples in Philippi ever since the arrival of the colonists from Thasos in the fourth century, are now known chiefly by the names of their Latin counterparts. The Roman religion of the early Empire had been largely hellenized and its gods remade in the image of the Homeric pantheon. Jupiter naturally enough holds pride of place, identified with the Greek Zeus; his altars bear the well-known epithets of Optimus Maximus, Fulmen, Conservator; we find him associated here with Mercury, there with Mars, sometimes also with a local Thracian god called Myndrytus. Mars, who alone has no Greek counterpart, appears in his two aspects of the god of agriculture, who is invoked to bestow abundant harvests upon the Italian peasants who till the fields; and the god of war—though in the minor role of the patron of the professional hunters who play their ferocious game with wild beasts in the arena. Juno, Minerva, Venus-Aphrodite, and nearly all the Olympians are represented, but most remarkable is the manifold identification of Artemis, not only with the Latin Diana (once entitled 'Minervian Diana') but above all with the Thracian Bendis, a huntress like herself and a moon-goddess. Five centuries earlier, Herodotus had remarked upon the Thracian devotion to Artemis (he was certainly speaking of Bendis under this name); and in the time of Paul she still commands the widest devotion. According to C. Picard, 'there is no doubt that this Artemis-Diana was a Latinized Bendis'. Among the lesser deities, we find Hercules, Cupid and Nemesis; and an important place is held by the Italian agricultural deities—Mars, Vertumnus, Liber (the Italian Bacchus), and Libera, and above all Silvanus, an Italian god of field and forest, patron of woodcutters and stonemasons. Of the foreign deities, the first place was held by Queen Isis (Isis Regina); the city was solemnly placed under her protection by the colonist-veterans of Antony, immediately after the victory of 42 B.C. She was followed by the Lord Sarapis, together with Horus-Harpocrates (identified with Apollo), and the jackal-headed Anubis; and the presence of Telesphorus, the attendant of Health and of the deified physician Asklepius, in her sanctuaries is a sign that the Egyptian deities were worshipped in their capacity of Healers and Saviours. Anatolia is represented chiefly by the moon-god Men and the great Asian mother-goddess Cotys-Cybele; and the mention of 'the Most High God' (*theos hypsistos*, θεὸς ὕψιστος) of the slave-girl's cry (Acts xvi. 17) certainly suggests Sabazios, who frequently receives this name. Finally, there was at Philippi a small community of worshippers of the God of Israel, of which we shall have more to say.

A highly significant feature of the religion of the period is the multiplication of private brotherhoods, cult-associations (*sodalitates, thiasoi*) devoted to the worship of a chosen god; and there were many such groups at Philippi. We hear of an association of worshippers (*cultores*) of Silvanus, another dedicated to the worship of Cybele and to the imperial cult at the same time. There are *mystai* of Dionysus, *thiasi* (the Greek term Latinized) of Father Liber, and *posiastae* of a Thracian god, unknown by name, who appears on many reliefs as a knight on horseback and receives the epithets of *Sōzōn* ('He who saves') and *Epēkoös* ('He who answers prayer'). Most of these groups at Philippi were burial-clubs, and several inscriptions tell of legacies received by them to provide for the care of the tomb and for the performance of annual rites in honour of the bene-factor. The rites themselves are in part transferred from Italy, and were performed at one of the ancient Italian seasons for the cult of the dead—either the *Rosalia* or the *Parentalia*; but other elements appear to be of Thracian origin, notably the Banquet—a communion of the dead—which is depicted upon many of the funerary reliefs, and a burnt offering of some kind. The ancient Thracian religious inheritance makes itself felt most strongly in this reinforcing of the cult of the dead and the hope of immortality. Thrace was of course the homeland of Dionysus and of his mysteries; and of Orpheus, the sweet singer who descended into the realm of Hades to bring back his beloved Eurydice from the dead, and all but succeeded. When Paul came to Philippi, he would find ready hearers for a gospel of resurrection from the dead, and life eternal.

There can be no doubt that the mission in Philippi was felt by Paul to be a new departure, the opening of a significant new adventure in the progress of the gospel. His earlier missions had been conducted in Semitic lands, where Greek culture had scarcely penetrated beneath the surface. Along the Asian coast, to be sure, he would have found Greek cities, established for centuries, which had attained a brilliant civilization long before the days of Athenian greatness. When he started westward from Lystra with Silas and the youthful Timothy, he may well have been projecting a mission in Ephesus or Miletus or any of the flourishing cities of Asia; but a divine admonition which he could not oppose forbade him to attempt it: they were 'forbidden by the Holy Spirit to preach the Word in Asia' (Acts xvi. 6). He would hardly have gone on to Troas, unless he had some thought in mind of taking ship for the West. It may even be that he was already entertaining the first dreams of planting the banner of Christ in Rome itself. In some sense, he must have thought of his coming to Philippi as the first great step in the campaign to win the world for Christ; for some years later, he can think of it as 'the beginning of the Gospel' (Phil. iv. 15) —a most extraordinary phrase, seeing that he himself had already been preaching in 'the regions of Syria and Cilicia' for at least fourteen years (Gal. i. 21; ii. 1), to say nothing of the activities of those who were apostles before him. At all events, the change from Syria and Cilicia, the scene of his earlier labours, and from the half-barbarian highlands of Galatia, meant that he was leaving the Oriental world—still deeply Oriental, in spite of a leavening of Greek influences; and entering the Greek world—still basically Greek, in spite of a growing infiltration of Oriental influences; and at Philippi in particular, he was making his first contacts with Romans other than administrators of a sullenly hostile territory, only recently subdued. Philippi must have seemed to him like the entrance to a new world, with new problems and new perspectives.

Nevertheless, his first approach is made through the Jewish community. The indications are that there were not many Jews in Philippi, for the missionaries spent 'some days' (in Acts, the phrase usually means a good many days) in the city without meeting any, and they seem to have followed somewhat vague directions when they at last found some worshippers gathered outside the gate, near the riverside, on a sabbath day. The story reads: 'We were spending some days in this city; and on the sabbath day we went outside the gate, along the river, where we thought that there was a place of prayer (*proseuchē*—

the word is sometimes used as a synonym for *synagōgē*, "synagogue", but not in the Lucan writings); and we sat down and spoke to the women who had gathered' (Acts xvi. 12-13). The fact that there were no men present is in itself evidence that very few Jews lived in the area; it was never a Jewish practice to leave attendance at public worship to the women of the family. The one woman who is specifically mentioned was not herself a Jewess by birth, probably not even a proselyte, but one of those 'God-fearing' Gentiles who had become attached in a more or less informal way to Judaism (see Arndt & Gingrich, *Lexicon*, s.v. σέβω; and *Beginnings of Christianity*, vol. v, Additional Note viii, 'Proselytes and God-fearers', by K. Lake). Lake remarks that 'this fringe of non-Jews, not satisfied with heathenism, and hesitating whether to become proselytes or to start some new method of worshipping God, provided the Christian missionaries with the best possible opportunity for making converts' (*op. cit.*), p. 77. This woman was from the city of Thyatira in Lydia, famous from Homeric times for its purple-dyeing industry; she was herself a merchant of purples, and the name by which she was known at Philippi—'Lydia'—was probably not her personal name but a nickname: 'the Lydian'. Her entire household was baptized with her; as the household of a prosperous business woman would include slaves and any other members of her establishment, it alone would make a fair nucleus of a Philippian congregation. A person such as Lydia would also provide the missionaries with the means of access to Gentiles quite unattached to Judaism, and thus widen the field of their labours.

Unfortunately, the book of Acts tells us nothing more of the mission proper, but passes on quickly to an account of the incident which led to the enforced departure of Paul and his companions. The masters of a slave-girl who made their livelihood by exploiting her powers of divination were enraged when Paul, by an exorcism in the name of Jesus Christ, caused her to lose her lucrative gift. As they could not make the expulsion of a 'spirit' (*pneuma*) of soothsaying the ground of an accusation, they charged Paul and Silas with sedition, playing at the same time upon the anti-semitic prejudices of their fellow-citizens: 'These men', they alleged, 'are stirring up trouble in our city,

Jews that they are; and are advocating customs which it is not lawful for us, as Romans, to observe' (xvi. 20-21). Abusive and unjust as they are, the words clearly presuppose that the apostles have not confined themselves to chats with a few women by the riverside or to quiet prayer-meetings in the house of Lydia! They would be utterly pointless if they did not rest upon the common knowledge that Paul and his company had been publicly seeking converts among the Gentiles—indeed, among the Romans—of Philippi. That is to say, they give a tantalizing hint of vigorous efforts to propagate the gospel in the city, of which the narrative contains no other trace.

The magistrates were perhaps already disquieted by what they had heard of the activity of the Christian preachers, and the townspeople showed hostility. The result was that Paul and Silas were flogged and thrown into prison, and the next morning were expelled from the city, with time only to say good-bye to Lydia and 'the brethren'—the converts, that is, who used her house as their centre. The story of the earthquake which opened the prison doors and loosed the fetters of the prisoners, of the converted jailor and the humble apologies offered by the magistrates has all the earmarks of legend. Far from being brought to offer abject apologies for flogging the apostles, the magistrates forced them to leave town the next morning. Writing to the Thessalonians a few months later, Paul still recalls the event with indignation. 'As you know,' he writes, 'we had suffered and been shamefully treated at Philippi before we came to you' (1 Thess. ii. 2).

The church at Philippi was solidly enough established to maintain itself, even in the absence of the apostles, in the face of the hostility which had driven away their leaders and must have continued to make itself felt against them. Nothing more is known of their life, except from occasional references in the letters of Paul himself, until the time that he wrote our epistle (or epistles). It has recently been argued that the letter known to us as 2 Thessalonians—which in fact is hard to explain as an authentic letter of St. Paul addressed to the *Thessalonian church* —was really sent to the Philippians not long after the enforced departure of the apostles (see the article of E. Schweizer, 'Der zweite Thessalonicherbrief ein Philipperbrief?' in *ThZ*, vol. i, no. 2 (August 1945), pp. 90-105). This suggestion deserves the most serious consideration, but until it has been more thoroughly debated, we cannot use that epistle as evidence for conditions in Philippi. One thing is certain, that the Christians of Philippi were not intimidated by the sufferings inflicted upon their apostles: within the weeks that followed, they twice sent supplies to Paul and his companions in Thessalonica (Phil. iv. 15, 16), and continued their aid during the mission in Corinth (2 Cor. xi. 8, 9). And Paul pays tribute to the generosity with which they, along with the other churches of Macedonia, contributed to his great collection for the poor of the Jerusalem church: 'at a time when they were severely tested by affliction, their over-flowing joy and their deep poverty were given overwhelming expression in the wealth of their liberality; for they gave according to their power and even—I bear them witness—beyond their power' (2 Cor. viii. 2, 3).

Paul was to visit Philippi twice more, towards the end of his career of free activity. The book of Acts merely mentions the fact that after a mission of more than two years in Ephesus, 'Paul resolved in the Spirit to proceed to Jerusalem, after a trip through Macedonia and Achaea', intending after that to see Rome also (Acts xix. 21). From his own letters, we learn that the purpose of the tour was to gather together the contributions of the different churches and to take them to Jerusalem, in fulfilment of his pledge to the 'pillars' of the mother church and in the hope of disarming the last opposition to the Gentile mission on the part of the Jewish Christians (Gal. ii. 10; Rom. xv. 25 ff.; 1 Cor. xvi. 1-9; 2 Cor. ix. 1-5). The troubles of the Corinthian church led him to hasten his journey. After the failure of several attempts to restore order by letter and through personal visitation, he had sent Titus to Corinth in a last, almost despairing effort to win them back. With him, he sent a most moving letter, part of which survives in the closing chapters of our 2 Corinthians, a letter which he wrote 'out of deep affliction and anguish of heart, with many tears' (2 Cor. ii. 4); and Titus, it appears, was to meet him at Troas on his return, with news of how his mission had fared. Paul, accordingly, went on from Ephesus to Troas, and began a promising work of evangelization there, but he was too much concerned

13

over the Corinthian situation to continue. As he tells us: 'When I had come to Troas for the gospel of Christ, even though a door stood open for me in the Lord I had no rest in my spirit because I did not find my brother Titus there; so I took leave of them and went on into Macedonia. . . . Even when we came into Macedonia our flesh had no rest but we were afflicted in every way—fights without, fears within. But God who comforts the lowly comforted us by the arrival of Titus' (2 Cor. ii. 12-13; vii. 5-6), with the best of news. Philippi is not mentioned by name—Paul makes a habit of thinking in terms of the provinces —but we cannot doubt that he would stop in Philippi with the friends to whom he was so deeply attached. His words may be taken, then, as giving us a glimpse of the Philippian church. 'Fights without, fears within': the inward fears may be his own cares occasioned by the trouble at Corinth; but the 'fights without' certainly suggests a church beset by foes. The early hostility of the crowd is still finding vent in attacks upon the Christians. The same difficult situation is probably reflected in his words (cited above) that they made their contribution to the collection for Jerusalem 'at a time when they were being severely tested by affliction'.

Paul went on to Corinth, as he had planned, and remained there for three months; after that, he abandoned his plan to go to Jerusalem by sea and decided instead to make the journey overland by way of Macedonia; and on this occasion, Acts tells us directly that he stayed in Philippi over the Passover season (Acts xx. 3, 5). Nothing more is known of this visit, which was to be his last. Soon after he reached Jerusalem, he was taken into custody by troops of the Roman garrison, to save him from death at the hands of a Jewish mob (Acts xxi. 30-32); and he remained a prisoner of the Romans, in all probability, until his death—a period of not less than five years.

No further information about the church of Philippi or about Paul's relations with it is available to us, except the little that can be gleaned from the epistle to the Philippians itself. From it we learn that this church had leaders called 'bishops' and 'deacons'; that it had sent gifts to the Apostle in his prison by the hand of one of their young men, called Epaphroditus, who had remained to do the prisoner what service he could. We learn the names of two women, Evodia and Syntyche, who have worked nobly for the gospel but are now threatening to cause trouble in the church through their rivalry; and we learn of one man, Clement (possibly of another called Syzygus), whom Paul mentions along with 'the rest of (his) fellow workers whose names are in the book of life' (Phil. iv. 2, 3). The Apostle has no rebukes for this church; he makes no suggestion that it is endangered by false doctrine of any kind; he makes it abundantly evident that he is deeply attached to all its members—he 'longs for them all in the heart of Christ Jesus' (i. 8); they are his 'beloved, for whom he deeply longs; his joy and crown'. The one warning that he has to give them is a warning against disunity; his one plea to them is that they should be one in disposition, one in soul and spirit, united in the service of Christ.

3. TIME AND PLACE OF WRITING

Until very recent times, it was universally agreed that the epistle to the Philippians was written at Rome, and the only question that seemed to require discussion was whether it should be regarded as the earliest or the latest of the epistles of the Roman imprisonment, to which Colossians, Philemon, and Ephesians were also assigned (so long as they were recognized as authentic). In the nineteenth century, however, some critics argued that all these epistles were more likely written from Caesarea; and in the twentieth century this view was still maintained by E. Haupt and E. Lohmeyer. Since 1900, it has been losing ground to a new hypothesis, first advanced by Adolf Deissmann in 1897 and now accepted by many scholars in Germany, Britain, France, and America, that Philippians and the other 'Imprisonment Epistles' were written at Ephesus. Some of Deissmann's followers accept this hypothesis for Philippians but not for Colossians and its companion epistles; and there is no need for us here to consider the question except in relation to Philippians. Many of the supporters of the Ephesian hypothesis seem inclined to favour it as a means for defending the authenticity of some few fragments of the Pastoral Epistles, if not the entire text; as the present writer sees no justification for allowing a line of them to St. Paul, he will not take their supposed evidence into consideration.

The Roman hypothesis has the advantage of age. It was current in the second century and was virtually unchallenged until the end of the eighteenth century. In a case such as this, however, tradition is far from decisive, even though unchallenged for so many centuries; for there is nothing to show that the earliest statements are based upon secure information. What is designated 'tradition' in these matters is very often nothing more than a second-century guess, repeated uncritically generation after generation. The case for a Roman provenance must stand or fall by the evidence to be drawn from the epistle itself. Such evidence may be summarily stated as follows:

(1) The references to 'the whole praetorium', or 'the whole praetorian guard', in i. 13; and to 'all the saints, especially those of the household of Caesar' in iv. 22. It is possible to give an interpretation of these allusions which would make them applicable to either Ephesus or Caesarea; but it must be admitted that the first and most natural impression of the reader is that they refer to Rome.

(2) The picture of rival groups, some moved by love for Paul and alive to his position as 'set for the defence of the gospel'; some moved by an unholy spirit of partisanship (i. 15-17). Such a situation is more readily understood of Rome than of either Caesarea or Ephesus. The epistle to the Romans indicates that the Apostle feared misunderstandings of his teaching among the Romans, and that he felt it necessary to guard against the possibility of resentment that he, as a stranger to them, should undertake to instruct them. Thus at the very beginning of his letter, he points out that the commission which he has received from Christ 'to promote obedience to the faith among *all* the nations' brings them also within the orbit of his apostolic responsibility (Rom. i. 5, 6; 14, 15). As soon as he has spoken of his desire to communicate to them some spiritual gift to strengthen them, he hastens to suggest that he is really thinking of *mutual* benefits to be given and received: 'that is, that we may be mutually encouraged when I am among you by our mutual faith' (i. 11-12). And again at the close (after the most

elaborate exposition of doctrine that has come down to us from his pen!), he assures them that he has no doubt that they already know everything that he could teach them, and that he has only written to them 'perhaps a trifle too boldly . . . by way of reminding you' again mentioning 'the grace given to me from God that I should be a minister of Christ Jesus to the nations' (xv. 14-16). And he still finds it necessary to insist that he has never made a habit of poaching on the preserves of other missionaries: he has been, on the contrary, 'ambitious to preach the gospel not where Christ had been named, lest I should build upon someone else's foundation' (xv. 20). It is quite conceivable that when he did come to Rome, he found that his misgivings were entirely and unhappily justified, for some of the local leaders (perhaps even more, some of their followers) were jealous of his transcendent gifts and great renown, and redoubled their activities with mixed motives, with a zeal that was not wholly pure. Such a state of affairs seems unlikely at Caesarea and impossible at Ephesus.

(3) The importance that Paul attaches to the clarification of the issues involved in his imprisonment. His case has served to further the progress of the gospel, precisely in that it has become known that his imprisonment is 'in Christ'; that is, that he is in fetters for the faith to which he is committed and not for disturbing the peace or for any kind of bad conduct. It is more likely that he would see his case as possessing such a high degree of significance if he were on trial in the supreme court of the Empire, than if he were merely appearing before a provincial official.

(4) The messenger from Philippi, Epaphroditus, has remained, and risked his life, to aid the Apostle. Would there be any need for this personal assistance at Ephesus, or for the gifts of the Philippians for that matter; seeing that Ephesus was the centre of a long and fruitful mission in the course of which 'all the inhabitants of Asia heard the word of the Lord, both Jews and Greeks' (Acts xix. 10; there are indications in the epistle to the Colossians that the cities of the Lycus valley, a hundred miles inland, were evangelized at this time; see Col. iv. 13)? And it is hard to believe that at Caesarea he would be so completely abandoned by the Jerusalem church, to which he

had just brought generous gifts from Macedonia and Achaea, that he would require aid from the Philippian church, twelve hundred miles away.

(5) It is known that Paul was imprisoned for at least two years in Rome, and in conditions which admitted of his receiving visitors and of 'preaching the kingdom of God and teaching the things concerning the Lord Jesus Christ with all freedom, without hindrance' (Acts xxviii. 30-31). It is not known that he was ever imprisoned in Ephesus; and it is by no means certain that at Caesarea he enjoyed the same liberty of action as at Rome. In Caesarea, he was imprisoned in 'the praetorium of Herod'; in Rome, he was allowed to live in his own rented dwelling. At Caesarea, moreover, he was in no danger of death; Felix would have released him at any time upon payment of a bribe (Acts xxiv. 26).

The arguments which have led a number of scholars to date the epistle many years earlier and to hold that it was written at Caesarea or at Ephesus may be briefly stated.

(i) The first place is usually given to considerations of distance, and the practical difficulty of so many journeys to and fro. The epistle presupposes four trips between Rome and Philippi, viz. (1) a message is sent from Rome to Philippi, with word that the Apostle is in prison; (2) Epaphroditus comes from Philippi to Rome, bringing gifts for the Apostle; (3) word is sent from Rome to Philippi that their messenger Epaphroditus has fallen sick; and (4) a message comes back from Philippi to Rome, saying that the Philippians have been distressed to learn of this illness. The return of Epaphroditus with the epistle would make a fifth journey; it is to be followed by the sending of Timothy; and Paul himself hopes to get back to Philippi not long afterwards. The distance between these two cities was nearly 800 miles. From Rome, a messenger would follow the Appian Way for 360 miles to Brundisium (Brindisi); he would then take ship across the Adriatic to Dyrrachium (Durazzo)—a two-day trip, provided the weather were favourable; and from Dyrrachium he would take the Egnatian Way for 370 miles to Philippi. Sir William Ramsay has calculated that the average distance of a day's travel overland, on foot, would not be above fifteen miles (*HDB*, v, art. 'Roads and

Travel (N.T.)', p. 386). At this rate, the one-way journey from Rome to Philippi would take over seven weeks; and if we allow the messenger to take a few days' rest between trips and perhaps to encounter an occasional delay along the way, we should have to allow something close to five months for the return trip, or about ten months for the four journeys which the letter implies had taken place before it was written. This period could be cut in half if we could suppose, as is not at all unreasonable, that the Philippians heard of Paul's appeal to Caesar soon after it was made, and sent their messenger on to Rome to meet him with supplies on his arrival. We should still have to allow four or five months for the exchanges of correspondence, before the despatch of the epistle. Since Paul was kept under guard in his own house at Rome for two years, there was clearly time enough for all these journeys; but it will be agreed that they would have been much less formidable, if it were only a matter of going from Ephesus to Philippi and back; this would take only ten or twelve days in each direction. The journey to Caesarea, on the other hand, involved a trip of over 1200 miles overland, and would certainly take much longer than the journey to Rome; for communications through Asia Minor were not equal under the best conditions to those between Rome and the Hellespont, and for several months in the winter, the roads over the Taurus mountains were impassable. The journey by sea would likewise take several weeks, if we may judge by the fact that Paul, leaving Philippi immediately after Easter, feels that he cannot take time to stop over in Ephesus if he is to be in Jerusalem for Whitsuntide (Acts xx. 16). The matter of distance, accordingly, gives some support to the Ephesian hypothesis, but tells rather against the Caesarean.

(ii) Paul tells us himself that after he had been to Rome he planned to undertake a mission in Spain (Rom. xv. 24, 28); whereas in Philippians he says that he will visit Philippi as soon as he is released from prison. This argument is singularly weak. When Paul wrote Romans, he was a free man, and at the height of his powers; it would not be strange if after five years in custody he would no longer have the impulse to start new work in strange territory, but would long to return to the Aegean cities to see his old friends once again.

(iii) It is alleged by Michaelis that the doubtful situation, which the Apostle feels may very well end in his execution, is not to be reconciled with the relatively easy conditions of the imprisonment mentioned in Acts xxviii. 30 f. But there is nothing extravagant in the supposition that after two years of *libera custodia* before his case came up for trial, Paul should find himself in a much less comfortable state. His first hearing may well have resulted in his transference to a prison, and made him realize that his appeal to Caesar was quite apt to issue in the pronouncement of the death sentence. But it must also be noted that he is still able to carry on his correspondence with his churches, and to make plans for his junior helpers, Timothy and Epaphroditus. If Paul ever was imprisoned in Ephesus, what makes the proponents of this hypothesis so sure that the conditions of that imprisonment were so mild as to allow this amount of apostolic activity?

(iv) Perhaps the most weighty part of the argument for Ephesus (and to a lesser degree for Caesarea) is that which appeals to the similarities between Philippians and the earlier letters—to the Thessalonians, the Galatians, the Romans, and the Corinthians; and the differences between it and Colossians and Ephesians. This argument of course loses most of its weight if we refuse to recognize the authenticity of Ephesians; and, in the judgment of the present writer, it has been amply demonstrated that Ephesians is in fact a pseudonymous work (E. J. Goodspeed, *The Key to Ephesians* [Chicago: U. of C. Press, 1956]; C. L. Mitton, *The Epistle to the Ephesians* [Oxford: Clarendon Press, 1951]; and F. W. Beare, 'The Epistle to the Ephesians: Introduction and Exegesis', in *The Interpreter's Bible*, vol. x [New York & Nashville: Abingdon Press, 1953], pp. 596 ff.). Even Colossians is doubtful in some degree; its authenticity is not so firmly established as to permit it to be employed positively to settle the date of Philippians, to say nothing of the fact that several of the scholars who affirm an Ephesian origin for Philippians hold that Colossians (and Ephesians, if they regard it as genuine) was written there also. But if we can agree that the comparison with Ephesians is irrelevant, since that epistle is the work of a later Paulinist and not of Paul himself, it will also be felt that Colossians does not affect the question, even if we are wholly convinced of its authenticity; for Colossians is perhaps more than any of the other letters an *écrit d'occasion*—its vocabulary and thought framed in reaction to the strange proto-Gnostic doctrine which had found a foothold in the Colossian church (cf. F. W. Beare, 'The Epistle to the Colossians: Introduction', sec. iv, 'The Colossian "Heresy"', in *The Interpreter's Bible*, vol. xi [New York & Nashville: Abingdon Press, 1955], pp. 137 ff.). But the literary relationships between Philippians and the other Pauline epistles have recently been subjected to a careful study by Professor C. L. Mitton, in connection with his enquiry into the authenticity of Ephesians, with the finding that 'there is little evidence of passages from the other letters exerting a sustained or a recurring influence in Philippians. . . . The parallels appear to be unrelated to each other' (*op. cit.* p. 114 f.; and see the tabulation of the relevant passages in his 'Appendix V: Parallels to Philippians in the Other Pauline Epistles', pp. 330-332). Thus it appears that no light can be thrown on the date of Philippians by any conspicuous degree of similarity to one group of the other epistles. There is nothing in the style or language to deter us from affirming that it is the latest of them all.

(v) Feine holds that the sharp attack on the Judaizers in chapter iii is not conceivable in an epistle written from Rome, for he holds that the controversy with the Judaizing faction was a passing episode in the Apostle's career, confined to the middle fifties when Galatians and the Corinthian letters were written, and no longer a live issue in the early sixties when he was at Rome. Of course, if we accept the position adopted in this commentary, that chapter iii is an interpolation, written at a different time and possibly even to different readers, it becomes unnecessary to take it into account in deciding the question of time and place of writing for the epistle as a whole. Even apart from that, it is by no means certain that Paul is attacking Judaizers in the blistering words of chapter iii; in spite of the parallels with 2 Corinthians, the opponents here envisaged may be non-Christian Jews, as indeed many of the commentators have held; and certainly the clash of the church with Judaism was no passing episode. But in fact it is not to be taken so lightly for granted that the controversy within the church over the problem of circumcision and the Law of Moses was so quickly settled as all that. Fifty years after the death of Paul, Ignatius is still warning against a Judaism taught by uncircumcised men (*To the Philadelphians*, vi. 1); his words can hardly be understood except of Judaistic tendencies within the church.

(vi) The references to the *praitorion* of i. 13 and to the saints 'of the house of Caesar' of iv. 22 can be readily enough understood of either Caesarea or Ephesus. 'The house of Caesar' is taken to mean the slaves and freedmen of the Imperial civil service, who would be found in every part of the Empire; and the *praitorion* was certainly used of Herod's official residence at Caesarea and probably also of the residence of the proconsul of Asia in Ephesus. Lohmeyer is sure that it must refer to Herod's praetorium at Caesarea (*Brief an die Philipper*, p. 41) or possibly at Corinth or Ephesus, certainly in a provincial city and not in Rome; on the ground that there is no contemporary evidence that the Praetorian Guard at Rome was charged with the guarding of prisoners sent to the high court from the provinces. Feine is equally sure that the word means not a building anywhere, but the Praetorian Guard itself; and he points out that there is evidence that a detachment of Praetorians was for a time stationed at Ephesus, but there is no trace of their presence at Caesarea. It scarcely needs to be said that the nine cohorts of the Praetorian Guard were usually concentrated at Rome, after Tiberius built them a great barracks; and any detachments found in a provincial capital would be nothing more than a guard of honour for the proconsul.

(vii) As far as Ephesus is concerned, it remains to be demonstrated that Paul was ever imprisoned in that city. No such imprisonment is mentioned in the narrative of Acts, and the supposition that he was imprisoned there is nothing more than a conjecture framed in order to make it possible to hold that Philippians, certainly written from prison, was written around A.D. 55, during Paul's mission in Asia. The conjecture appeals to fragments of evidence from Paul's other letters, especially 2 Corinthians, which are not always susceptible of a clear and definite interpretation. Negatively, it is pointed out that Acts does not record all the imprisonments of Paul; in 2 Corinthians, written before or at the time of his second visit to Philippi, he affirms that he has been in jail more often than his opponents (xi. 23); the only imprisonment mentioned in Acts up to that point is the imprisonment at Philippi itself. Positively, Paul refers to terrible afflictions which he underwent in Asia, to the point that he despaired of life itself (2 Cor. i. 8), and again he speaks of having 'fought with beasts at Ephesus' (1 Cor. xv. 32). If the latter phrase must be taken literally, there is no doubt about the imprisonment, for only a prisoner under sentence would be sent into the arena to fight with the wild beasts. But there are two objections to taking the words literally. First, this is not a form of punishment to which a Roman citizen would be liable; and second, the victim of such an ordeal was unlikely to come out of it alive. Further, we may well doubt whether Ephesus possessed an arena in which these combats with wild animals could be staged. The Greek theatre was not designed for such use, and it was not until the second century, in most places, that the necessary remodelling was undertaken. It seems probable, therefore, that the 'wild beasts' with whom Paul fought at Ephesus were men.

It is fair to say, none the less, that it is possible that Paul was in prison for a time at Ephesus, in spite of the failure of Acts to mention it; but it cannot be taken to have been demonstrated. Further, even if we had much more conclusive evidence of such an imprisonment, it would remain to be shown that it was long enough to allow for the four trips between Ephesus and Philippi, and for the serious illness of Epaphroditus and his recovery— that is to say, not less than three months. It must also be shown that the conditions of the imprisonment were such as to allow the Apostle to receive friends, to direct the movements of his associates, and to receive and write letters. Let us remember that the writing of letters involves the admission of a scribe to the prison and the provision of papyrus at the prisoner's expense. It was not every prisoner who would be free to turn his cell into an executive office for the propagation of a religion of doubtful legality! It must be emphasized again that it is only for Rome that we have documentary evidence for a prolonged imprisonment which allowed Paul such freedom for his apostolic activities.

(viii) It is alleged by Michaelis that the epistle presupposes that Paul has been in Philippi only once in his life. This appears to be a quite unwarranted conclusion.

Taking everything into account, the ancient hypothesis that Philippians was written from Rome must be allowed to hold the field. A precise date cannot be established. We must be content to place it between 60 and 64, probably towards the later date.

'The Philippians are Macedonians. These, having received the word, stood firm in the faith and did not receive false apostles. The Apostle praises them, writing to them from Rome, from prison, by Epaphroditus.' (The [Latin] Marcionite prologue to the epistle, dating from the second century.)

4. CHARACTER, CONSTRUCTION, AND CONTENTS

It has been indicated above that we regard the epistle to the Philippians as a compilation, containing parts of three letters. of the Apostle Paul which were written on different occasions and one of them possibly to a different group of readers. We take the interpolated fragment of iii. 2 to iv. 1 to be the earliest part of the book. It may well have been composed at the time when the controversy with the Judaizers was at its height, which would make it roughly contemporary with Galatians, perhaps about A.D. 55. The other two letters we take to have been written from Rome; one of them, itself an interpolation in the other (iv. 10-20), sent to thank the Philippians for their gifts as soon as Epaphroditus delivered them—that is, at or near the beginning of Paul's imprisonment; the other, which forms the framework of the whole (i. 1-iii. 1; iv. 2-9, 21-23), written towards the end of the Apostle's life, charged with calm and quietly joyful premonitions of approaching death, and intended to be carried by Epaphroditus on his return journey to Philippi. Each of the three parts must be described separately.

(1) *The Interpolated Fragment*, iii. 2-iv. 1. It is impossible to arrive at any certainty about the destination of this fragment, or about the time and place of writing. It begins abruptly with a searing denunciation of Jewish, or possibly Jewish-Christian missioners; but its great interest lies in the manner in which

Paul is led to unfold the secrets of his own inward life, in contrast with the principles of religion in which he had been reared. In a most moving passage of spiritual autobiography, he tells us how he has renounced all that he once counted dear, for the sake of Christ; how he has made it the whole aim of his life 'to win Christ and be found in him . . . to know him and the power of his resurrection and fellowship of his sufferings, being continually conformed to his death' (iii. 7-10); how, like a runner in the stadium, he 'speeds on towards the finish line', not for any earthly prize, but for the heavenly guerdon to which God has called him in Christ (13-14). This is one of the principal sources of inspiration of Christian ascetical theology, and has been especially dear to the master teachers of the religious orders, especially in the Orthodox churches of Eastern Christendom.

The second section of our fragment begins with a denunciation of 'enemies of the cross of Christ', who are self-indulgent libertines and even boast of their shameful conduct (18-19). Paul contrasts with them and their mean concern for 'earthly things', the upward gaze of the Christian believer, and his expectation of a Saviour from heaven, who will transform his faithful followers into his glorious likeness (20-21).

(2) *The Letter of Thanks* iv. 10-20. This consists wholly of a remarkable acknowledgment of the gifts which Epaphroditus has brought to Paul from Philippi, together with the assurance that the Apostle is now amply supplied with all that he needs. Its most striking feature, however, is his affirmation of an independence of outward circumstances, an indifference to wealth and poverty, abundance and hunger, for which he actually uses the Stoic word αὐτάρκης—'self-sufficient', but with the confession—wholly alien to Stoicism—that his powers to remain undisturbed by changes of fortune are not his own, but are imparted to him by Christ.

(3) *The Final Letter*, i. 1-iii. 1; iv. 2-9, 21-23. This is probably the last of Paul's extant letters, and is in a sense his farewell message to the church militant here on earth. Its central message is a call for unity and steadfastness, and for a clear and unwavering witness to truth and goodness. It is perhaps the most intensely personal of all Paul's letters, reflecting from

beginning to end the deep and warm affection which binds him to the Christian community of Philippi. His affairs have come to a critical point; the issues have been made clear, in that it is known that he is on trial for his faith and not for any criminal activity; but the verdict is uncertain. At times, he writes as if he entertained good hopes of release, to permit the continuance of his work; but the prevailing impression is that he anticipates death, and is eager to prepare his beloved Philippians to carry on the struggle without him. In this respect, the letter is a classic utterance of the mind of the martyr, even though Ernst Lohmeyer has carried through much too sweepingly the theme of martyrdom.

The letter begins with a salutation (i. 1-2), and thanksgiving for the readers (3-5), followed by warm assurances of his affection for them and confidence in their future salvation (6-8), and a prayer for their spiritual growth (9-11). After these introductory paragraphs, the Apostle gives a brief account of the situation at Rome: his imprisonment has helped to further the good cause in that its true reason is now understood in responsible quarters, and in that it has encouraged others to bold and vigorous activity (12-14). Not all of those who have been spurred into action are moved by the purest of motives; some of them even imagine that they are hurting him; but Paul can only be glad that the gospel is being proclaimed, whatever the motives of the preachers (15-18). He turns now to his own outlook and expectations. Counting on their prayers, and on the resources that the Spirit of God will supply in answer, he has every hope that he will not weaken under whatever ordeal he may have to endure. He faces the prospect of death without fear, even with a measure of longing 'to move on and to be with Christ', which is countered only by his recognition that if he were destined to remain in the flesh, he could still be helpful to his churches; and this leads him to feel that he will be permitted to stay upon earth 'to further [their] progress and joy in the faith' (19-26).

This account of the local situation and the personal outlook of the Apostle is followed by a series of exhortations (i. 27-ii. 18). He bids them live as befits followers of Christ's gospel by manifesting a complete unity of mind and heart, in utter fearlessness of the dangers that threaten them (i. 27-30). He makes a most earnest plea for mutual love and concord, for the re-nunciation of all selfish ambition, and for the spirit that is more concerned to vindicate the rights and to esteem the qualities of others than to assert its own claims (ii. 1-4). Thus alone will they reflect in the life of their community the dispositions that belong to their union with Christ, the Lord of all, who has been exalted to the highest station in the universe after renouncing his divine glories and dignities and submitting in slave-like obedience to the lowly lot of man (ii. 5-11). A third exhortation (ii. 12-18) is modelled upon the parting charge of Moses to the Israelites whom he had led to the borders of the Promised Land (Deut. xxxi. 24 f., xxxii, 1 f.); he recalls their past obedience and encourages them to persevere until they have entered upon their eternal heritage ('work out your own salvation'), with the assurance of God's unfailing help. If he must die, let them think of his life as a sacrifice offered to God, and rejoice with him as he rejoices with them.

The Apostle now speaks of his arrangements for future work. He plans to send Timothy to Philippi as soon as possible, and pays him high tribute for his disinterested services to Christ and the church; and he expresses some hope that he may be able to visit them himself shortly afterwards (19-24). But he has decided to send Epaphroditus back to them at once, in view of the anxieties which have been aroused by his serious illness, of which they have heard; and he asks them to give their returning envoy the warmest of welcomes (25-30).

At this point he begins to say his farewells (iii. 1); but stops to add a direct appeal to the two women who have been the centres of disunity in the Philippian community; and he invites a 'true comrade' to help them compose their differences (iv. 2-3). Within this appeal, the editor of the correspondence has inter-polated the fragment iii. 2-iv. 1. Paul is now ready to resume his words of farewell (iv. 4), and he adds some parting counsels and assurances (iv. 5-9). At this point, the earlier letter of thanks is inserted (iv. 10-20); and following that, the main letter is brought to its conclusion with a few words of greeting from Paul and his friends at Rome to the Christians of Philippi (21-22); and a sentence of blessing (23).

EPISTLE TO THE PHILIPPIANS

The structure of the letter, as it has been transmitted to us, may be set forth as follows:

I. A Letter Sent with Epaphroditus on his Return to Philippi.

    A. Introductory Section. i. 1-11.

        1. The Salutation. i. 1-2.
        2. The Thanksgiving, with the Apostle's Assurances of his Affection. i. 3-8.
        3. A Prayer for the Philippians. i. 9-11.

    B. A Report on the Apostle's Situation and Prospects. i. 12-26.

        4. The Effects of his Imprisonment on the Local Church: New Vigour and Boldness. i. 12-17.
        5. The Apostle's Attitude and Outlook. i. 18-26.

    C. Exhortations to Unity. i. 27-ii. 18.

        6. First Exhortation: An Appeal for Unity and Fearlessness in the Face of the Enemies of the Gospel. i. 27-30.
        7. Second Exhortation: The Appeal for Unity in the Common Life, grounded in self-abnegation and concern for others. ii. 1-4.
        8. A Hymn to Christ, Humiliated and Glorified, the Lord of all Creation. ii. 5-11.
        9. Third Exhortation: The Apostle's Farewell Appeal. ii. 12-18.

    D. Announcement of Plans. ii. 19-30.

        10. The Apostle Hopes to Send Timothy, and to come later himself; Epaphroditus is returning at once, and the Apostle commends him highly. ii. 19-30.

    E. Conclusion and Postscript (commenced). iii. 1.

II. An Interpolated Fragment. iii. 2-iv. 1.

        11. A Warning against Jewish Propaganda: Paul's Renunciation of Judaism, and Devotion to Christ. iii. 2-16.
        12. A Warning against Libertines. iii. 17-iv. 1.

I. E. Conclusion and Postscript (continued).

        13. Personal Appeals, and Farewell Greetings and Counsels. iii. 1b; iv. 2-9.

---

5. THEOLOGY AND 'SPIRITUALITY'[1]

The epistle to the Philippians is the most personal of all Paul's letters, except perhaps for the little letter to Philemon. It contains no formal instruction, and nothing resembling an exposition of Christian doctrine. What it offers in the way of ethical appeal and exhortation is cast in the most general terms: to live worthily of Christ's gospel, to be united in mind and spirit, to be considerate and humble, to trust God and to make our requests known to him in prayer, and to keep our minds fixed on all that is true and noble and commendable. The Apostle assumes that his readers have no need of further indoctrination in the principles of the Christian faith or in the moral standards by which men should live; he is concerned chiefly to promote among them a steadfast devotion and a continual deepening of their inward life, to hold before them the vision of high and heavenly things and to awaken immortal longings in their hearts. He reveals to them the springs of his own spiritual life and invites them to imitate his devotion.

Even the great Hymn to Christ (ii. 6-11), which is one of the cardinal scriptural statements for the dogmatic theologian, is not primarily a formulation of Christological doctrine but a recital of the saving actions of Christ, put before us as the motive power of Christian living; it is less instructive than evocative. Considered as a doctrinal declaration, it is enigmatic; the meaning of its central phrases is not self-evident, but requires to be interpreted by the aid of other passages in the writings of the Apostle. Its words presuppose and imply a highly developed Christology, but cannot be said to unfold it. The underlying

[1] The term 'spirituality' is used here in the sense of the French 'spiritualité'—of all that bears upon the spiritual life; the quest of the Highest, and the disciplines which promote its attainment.

Christology, with which the readers are assumed to be well acquainted, includes the doctrine of a Christ pre-existent in heavenly glory in the form of God, who renounces his prerogative of equality with God (unlike others who sought impiously to seize the highest place) to take upon him the servile condition of humanity, and to die; and who has therefore been exalted by God to the supreme rule of his whole creation, and acclaimed as Lord by the spirit-powers who have held sway over its three realms—heaven, earth, and world below—but are now made subject to him who had accepted the thraldom of life in the human condition. This hymn is clearly cast in terms of myth, and that, a myth which makes use of the ancient picture of the universe as geocentric, and inhabited by mighty spirits in its triple structure. The notion of salvation which underlies it is essentially the liberation of mankind from the tyranny of these dark powers. The myth itself is in its primary formulation pre-Christian, and has its parallels in the redemption-mythology of Babylonia and Persia and in the stories of the apotheosis of heaven-born Heroes among the Greeks; it belongs to the great international treasure of mythology which was available at the period and was employed in the service of all manner of cults with the modifications appropriate to each. It is now held by many scholars that the hymn itself is a *pre-Pauline* Christian construction; but even though it seems probable that Paul was not himself the composer, it is difficult to imagine that the Gentile churches of Syria, in the few years (perhaps only months) of their existence before his conversion, could have advanced so far beyond the circle of their Judaic inheritance as to sing of Christ in such terms as these. It seems much more likely that the hymn is the work of a disciple of Paul's, and that the teaching of Paul is the middle term between the primitive Christology of the Jerusalem church and this bold adaptation to Jesus of the Oriental myth of the Descent of the Redeemer. By incorporating it into his letter, Paul has made it clear that he recognized in it a true and worthy statement of his gospel.

But whatever the source of the hymn and whoever may have been its composer, it is evident that it cannot be employed directly as a statement of Christian doctrine in our day—not because we have liberated our minds from myth, but because the presuppositions of this myth are too far removed from anything of which our imaginations are capable. We do not think of the universe in terms of a three-story construction, nor do we conceive the powers that affect its movements in terms of personal spirits capable of acclaiming Jesus as Lord at his enthroning. The thought requires to be translated, not merely from Greek into English, but from forms that were intelligible in the Hellenistic world of the first century into forms that have meaning for the Western world of the twentieth century. Much of the richness of the imagery will inevitably be lost, for there is some reduction involved in any attempt to relate the mythopoetic language of the hymn to the propositions of a doctrinal theology. We can discern here the doctrine of the pre-existence of our Lord, not as an impersonal Wisdom or Logos, but as a personal essence capable of choice that can in some sense be qualified as moral; the doctrine also of his incarnation, in terms of the renunciation of the most glorious condition of existence (described as 'being in the form of God') by a voluntary acceptance of the lowly condition of man (described as 'taking the form of a slave' and 'being found in fashion as a man'). Even these phrases are capable of being understood in more than one sense, and it is only by analogy with the entire theology of Paul (and of the New Testament and the church, for that matter), that we find in them a true doctrine of incarnation. Indeed, we give them an intelligible meaning of any kind only by bringing them into relation with some body of doctrine more comprehensive than that which they contain in themselves. Again, in the final strophe of the hymn, the Lordship of Christ is depicted in terms wholly of the homage paid to him by the spirit-rulers of the threefold universe; that is to say, the redemption accomplished by Christ is conceived in terms of victory over the demons who have held our human life in a state of thraldom. To the first century, this was a powerful conception, and it may well still be powerful in societies that are demon-ridden; but it is only by a forceful antiquarianizing that we can make ourselves in our Western world think of the hidden powers that affect the life of mankind in terms of 'angels and principalities and powers' which have been made subject to Christ in his Ascension (cf.

1 Peter iii. 22). Here we should have to reshape the thought in a most radical way, and may find it quite impossible to give it any kind of propositional form. We shall indeed hold to the confession that God raised our Lord Jesus from the dead and gave him glory; that God has given to him all authority in heaven and in earth; that he is able to set us free from every kind of bondage; and we shall gladly join in the acclamation, which we believe will one day be universal, that 'Jesus Christ is Lord', and that through him all God's creation renders to God the glory due unto his Name.

We shall feel, then, that there is some measure of justification for the words of F. C. Porter about 'this hymn to Christ, which only incites our curiosity about its origin, and its relationship to Jewish or heathen conceptions, but adds nothing to our knowledge of Jesus' (*The Mind of Christ in Paul*, p. 220). Despite the fascination which it has had for the theologians, the hymn not only 'adds nothing to our knowledge of Jesus', but contributes very little to our understanding of the mystery of his Person, the mystery of the Word made flesh. Its total theological significance has been consistently overestimated. Nevertheless, its influence on the history of Christian thought has undoubtedly been great, at all periods. To this we must add that much of its most persistent influence has been based upon misunderstanding; in the age of the Christological controversies, by the interpretation of *morphē* ('form' [of God]) in ontological terms, as if it were equivalent to *ousia* ('being', 'essence', substance'), whereas in fact it is not used metaphysically at all; and in modern times by the fantastic interpretations given to the phrase 'he "emptied" himself' ('stripped himself', in our translation; 'made himself of no reputation', in AV). On this, see Dr. Fairweather's Appended Note on 'The "Kenotic" Christology'.

Much more faithful to the sense in which Paul has used the hymn is the 'Kenoticism' of Russian spirituality, which has seen in the humiliated Christ, renouncing his divine and heavenly glory to dwell among men in the form of a slave, the pattern of life consecrated to God. For the hymn is in fact introduced by Paul in the context of his appeal to the Philippians to renounce any claims to honour or privilege that they may feel to be their due, all promptings of ambition, all self-assertiveness, and in humility to esteem others better than themselves. He does not point to Jesus in his infinite qualitative difference from man, as the resplendent heavenly being who descends briefly from his high estate and returns again exalted to the highest dignity; but lays all the emphasis on that in which Jesus can be imitated by man—on renunciation, self-abasement, identification with creatures of an infinitely lower estate than himself. To quote again the words of F. C. Porter: 'Whatever the writer of the hymn may have meant by these words, Paul meant, when he quoted them, not something peculiar to Jesus, involved in the fact that for him alone among men the earthly life must be somehow adjusted to his former and still essentially divine nature, but something that every Christian should repeat in his own choices and actions. To empty oneself was to have the self-less mind of one who counts others better than himself. What Paul wanted his readers to see in the poem was only what he had been urging them to be and do. To Paul it was a hymn in praise of the humility and self-sacrifice of Jesus, and pictured God's recognition of the beauty and glory of these qualities by enthroning as Lord him in whom they were revealed in their true nature' (op. cit. pp. 209-210). Paul does not bring the hymn before them as a statement of the divine and human natures of Christ, of the relation between the two natures in him or of the relation between him and the Father; these weighty theological problems are not in his mind. He is concerned with the life of the Christian community, that it should be penetrated through and through by the sentiments and disposition which befit those who are 'in Christ Jesus' and who live by participation in his life.

Important as this passage has been in the history of Christian thought, a still greater significance attaches to the epistle in the history of Christian spirituality. The springs and aspirations of the Christian life, its hopes and its resources, are here unfolded for us in a manner that has contributed mightily to the whole shape and character of Christian piety from the beginning and which has lost none of its compelling instructiveness for us in our time. Paul is not a theologian by choice or by design; he deals with theological questions only because they force themselves upon him in direct relation to his pastoral and evangelistic duties. In all his writings, theology is secondary to religion. As Father Bonsirven remarks, 'We have to do with a profoundly religious soul, who seeks to give an account, for himself and for his readers, of the supernatural life by which they are animated' (*L'Évangile de Paul* [Paris: Aubier, 1948], p. 34). When he speaks of his own religious experience and outlook, it is not for him the peculiar spiritual adventure of a virtuoso, but the personal manifestation in him of the life that is open to every Christian believer; so that without the slightest touch of vanity, he can propose himself as a pattern for the imitation of his readers. He makes no boast of himself, but only of Christ Jesus; what he is, he is by the grace of God communicated to him through Christ in the fellowship of his church, and available likewise to every disciple of Christ. He can speak of all his readers as 'co-partners' (συγκοινωνούς) of his grace (i. 7). He gladly acknowledges that he has nothing which he has not received, and he is only eager that others should open their hearts to the same divine grace in the fullest measure. He will be content with nothing less than 'to present every man perfect in Christ Jesus' (Col. i. 28).

For Paul, the Christian life is a participation in the life of Christ himself. 'To me to live is Christ', he tells us (i. 21), not meaning to lay claim to an unusual degree of devotion to his Master, but to confess the faith and affirm the love that belongs to the Christian as such. His readers are 'the saints in Christ Jesus who are at Philippi'; the 'harvest of righteousness' which he prays they may bring forth is given 'through Jesus Christ' (i. 11); they are suffering 'for Christ's sake' (i. 29); like Paul, they 'take pride [only] in Christ Jesus' (iii. 3), and live expectantly, awaiting his coming from heaven as Saviour (iii. 20). His appeals and exhortations, his prayers and his hopes, are all made 'in the Lord', 'in Christ Jesus', 'in Christ'; and if he has learned to endure, to have strength for every trial, he knows that the source of this strength is not in himself, but in Christ: 'I have strength for all, in him who empowers me' (iv. 13).

The new life of the Christian believer is not an achievement of his own, but a work of God; and its continuance rests upon the assurance that God will finish what he has himself begun:

'He who began a good work in you will carry it to completion, until the Day of Christ' (i. 6). We are encouraged to work out our own salvation by the recollection that God is at work among us, that we may both in will and in deed fulfil his good pleasure (ii. 13). The harvest of righteousness which our lives are to bring forth through Jesus Christ redounds to his glory and praise (i. 11). We are his children, set by him in the world like stars, to give the pure light of his truth in the midst of a corrupt society (ii. 15-16). By continual converse with him in prayer we are to find the secret of freedom from anxiety, for his peace will guard our hearts and thoughts through Christ Jesus (iv. 6-7). We are promised that he will supply every need of ours out of his boundless wealth; and to him, our God and Father, belongs the glory eternal (iv. 19-20).

The promised fulfilment of the new life which God has given to us is nothing less than transformation into the likeness of Christ. This final goal will only be attained in its completeness at the Resurrection, at 'the Day of Christ' of which Paul speaks again and again, at his coming from heaven as our Saviour, awaited by his followers with expectation and longing (iii. 11, 21). Elsewhere in his letters, Paul speaks of a *progressive* transformation of the Christian believer: 'All of us, with unveiled face mirroring the glory of the Lord, are being transformed into the same image from glory to glory, as by the Lord, the Spirit' (2 Cor. iii. 18). Or again he can exhort us to be transformed: 'I beseech you . . . be transformed by the renewing of the mind, that you may prove in practice what is the will of God—good, wellpleasing, perfect' (Rom. xii. 2). In our epistle, he is concerned rather to depict for us the manner of his own life in its singleminded aspiration towards the attainment of this goal. He is animated by the most ardent love of Christ; the knowledge of Christ Jesus his Lord is the supreme good, for which he has cast away all that he once prized and all else that the world deems precious (iii. 7-8). Even in prison, faced with the menace of death, he has no concern save that he may maintain his loyalty to Christ; it is his eager expectation and hope that now as always Christ shall be magnified in his body, whether it be by his life or by his death (i. 20). His whole being is filled with the one desire, that he may win Christ and be found in him

(iii. 8-9). He has no thought that he can ever *deserve* so great a blessing, as if it could be earned by a high level of moral achievement; he disavows any claim to a righteousness of his own, based on the keeping of God's Law, which might in any degree entitle him to the divine favour (iii. 9)—that belongs to the way of life in which he once took pride as a devout Pharisee, but which he now reckons as a liability, not an asset (iii. 4-7). He is now concerned only with that righteousness 'which is given through faith in Christ, the righteousness which proceeds from God and is accorded to faith' (iii. 9). The knowledge of Christ for which he seeks is the knowledge of shared experience—that the mystical reality of union with Christ may be deepened and as it were made actual through 'the power of his resurrection', experienced as the power which rules in Paul's own life; that the sufferings which he undergoes in his struggle for the advance of the gospel may be so fused with the sufferings of Christ as to weld ever stronger the bonds of fellowship that bind him to his Master; that he may, by the daily mortifying of all that is earthly in him, conform himself to Christ's death (iii. 10), and so at last attain to the resurrection from the dead (iii. 11). The death with Christ which he has undergone in baptism (Rom. vi. 2 ff.), in one sense accomplished, is now viewed as an experience that must be continually renewed: the old corrupt nature, crucified with Christ, must still be made to perish. As he puts it in another place, we must have the sentence of death within ourselves, and must be continually bearing about in our body the dying of Jesus, in order that the life of Jesus also may be manifested in our body (2 Cor. i. 9, iv. 10).

To the attainment of the ultimate goal, he devotes himself with unremitting energy. He depicts himself as a runner in the stadium, never looking back over his shoulder to congratulate himself on the amount of ground he has already covered, but thinking only of the stretch of track that lies still ahead, and speeding on to the finishing post, that he may be awarded the prize of the winner (iii. 12-14). He counts nothing accomplished until the race has been won and the prize received—the prize of the high calling of God in Christ Jesus. And this is the approach to life which he commends to all (iii. 15).

For such a life, death has no terrors. If 'to live is Christ', then 'to die is gain'; and Paul voices his longing 'to move on and to be with Christ, for that is far and away better' (i. 21, 23). If there is any division in his mind, it is not occasioned by any doubt that the life to come is more desirable than this, but only by his sense of the services which he can still do for his churches (i. 24-25). In the same spirit, he has also written to the Corinthians: 'Therefore, always highhearted and knowing that while we are at home in the body we are absent from the Lord—for we live by faith, not by sight—we are, I say, always highhearted and are ready and willing to depart from the body and to take up our home with the Lord' (2 Cor. v. 6-8). He does not attempt to suggest to us in any way how he envisages this state into which the Christian enters at death, except for his assurance that it is 'far and away better'. It is still not the final beatitude of knowing as he is known, of seeing face to face, of being transformed wholly into the likeness of Christ; for that, he must await the coming of the Lord from heaven (iii. 21). It is an intermediate state, still less than the fullness of redemption, which must include 'the redemption of the body' (Rom. viii. 23). It is still a state of expectation; yet it clearly brings with it a deliverance from the burden of the flesh, and a greater closeness of communion with Christ, so that it can be described as being 'with Christ' in a sense that does not apply to our life in the present age. And the final salvation is not for him a distant event. 'The Lord is at hand' (iv. 5). He has no thought of the long perspective of history, and it would never occur to him to think more particularly of the nature of the intermediate state, since it will endure only briefly, until with the Parousia of the Lord, death is swallowed up in victory (1 Cor. xv. 54); and we that have borne the image of the earthly, shall bear eternally the image of the heavenly Man, Christ Jesus (1 Cor. xv. 49).

6. BIBLIOGRAPHY

I. COMMENTARIES

(A) *English Language*

Lightfoot, J. B., *St. Paul's Epistle to the Philippians: A Revised Text, with Introduction, Notes, and Dissertations*. London:

Macmillan & Co., 1868; 4th edition revised, 1885; many reprints.

Meyer, H. A. W., *Critical and Exegetical Commentary on the New Testament*, Part IX, 'The Epistles to the Philippians and Colossians', 4th edition, trans. by J. C. Moore and W. P. Dickson. Edinburgh: T. & T. Clark, 1885.

Michael, J. H., *The Epistle of Paul to the Philippians*, in the *Moffatt New Testament Commentary*. London: Hodder & Stoughton, 1928; several reprints.

Scott, E. F., 'The Epistle to the Philippians: Introduction and Exegesis', in *The Interpreters' Bible*, vol. xi. New York and Nashville: Abingdon, 1955. Exposition by R. F. Wicks.

Vincent, M., *The Epistles to the Philippians and to Philemon*, in the *International Critical Commentary*. Edinburgh: T. & T. Clark, 1897. Several reprints.

(B) *Foreign Languages*

Barth, K., *Erklärung des Philipperbriefes*. Zürich: Zollikon, 1927. Several reprints.

Bonnard, P., *L'Épître de saint Paul aux Philippiens*, in the *Commentaire du Nouveau Testament*. Neuchâtel: Delachaux & Nestlé, 1950.

Dibelius, M., *An die Thessalonicher I-II. An die Philipper*, in H. Lietzmann's *Handbuch zum Neuen Testament*, 11. 3rd ed. rev. Tübingen: Mohr, 1937.

Ewald, P., *Der Brief des Paulus an die Philipper*, 4th ed. rev. by G. Wohlenberg; in T. Zahn's *Kommentar zum Neuen Testament*, XI. Leipzig and Erlangen: Deichert-Scholl, 1923.

Haupt, E., 'Der Brief an die Philipper', in *Die Gefangenschaftsbriefe*; in Meyer's *Kritisch-exegetischer Kommentar*, Pt. IX, 7th ed. Göttingen: Vandenhoeck & Ruprecht, 1902.

Lohmeyer, E., 8th edition of the preceding, 1930. 11th edition, 1955. (The later editions are little altered from the 8th.)

Lueken, W., 'Der Brief an die Philipper', in *Die Schriften des Neuen Testaments*, vol. ii, 3rd ed., ed. W. Bousset and W. Heitmüller. Göttingen: Vandenhoeck & Ruprecht, 1917.

Michaelis, W., *Der Brief an die Philipper*, in *Theologisches Handkommentar zum Neuen Testament*, 11. Leipzig: Deichert, 1935.

I have ventured to make use of a few sentences from Erasmus' 'Paraphrasis in Epistolam Pauli ad Philippenses', from J. LeClerc's edition, *Opera Omnia*, vol. vii, Leiden: Van der Aa, 1706.

Attention must also be drawn to the Novisad conference of 1929:

'Ostwestliche Theologenkonferenz in Novisad vom 3. bis 10. August, 1929: Der Philipperbrief', reported in *Theologische Blätter*, Jg. 8, No. 11 (November 1929). The chief interest of this conference lies in its ecumenical character; it brought together representatives of Western Protestantism and Eastern Orthodoxy, with such distinguished contributors as M. Dibelius, P. Bratsiotis, K. L. Schmidt, K. Beth, N. Glubokowsky, H. Clavier, S. Besobrasoff, C. H. Dodd, F. Bednar, W. Michaelis, and Bishop Irenaeus of Novisad, the Chairman. The Orthodox theologians generally emphasized aspects of the epistle which are seldom noted in Western commentaries, particularly its historic importance for Ascetical Theology, for the monastic Rules, and for the piety of the Eastern church generally.

II. SPECIAL STUDIES

(A) *On the Time and Place of Writing*

The hypothesis that Philippians was written by St. Paul from Ephesus was first put forward by Adolf Deissmann in lectures at Herborn in 1897. Since then it has been the subject of numerous essays and articles. It has won the acceptance of many good scholars, but many remain inclined to hold to the tradition of a Roman origin, and a few (notably E. Haupt and E. Lohmeyer) have maintained that it was written from Caesarea. The literature is extensive. A bibliography of the most important contributions published before 1925 is given in A. Deissmann's *St. Paul: A Study in Social and Religious History* (2nd ed., trans. W. E. Wilson [London: Hodder & Stoughton, 1926]), pp. 17 ff.

In English, the Ephesian hypothesis has been supported chiefly by G. S. Duncan in his book *St. Paul's Ephesian Ministry* (London: Hodder & Stoughton, 1929), which Professor C. H. Dodd has called 'the only really thorough presentation of it in English'; it is adopted by J. H. Michael in his commentary on Philippians; and had earlier received the support of such distinguished scholars as B. W. Bacon, C. R. Bowen, Kirsopp Lake, and others. The most thorough criticism in English is that offered by Dodd in his essay, 'The Mind of Paul: II', most recently published in *New Testament Studies* (Manchester: Manchester University Press, 1953); partly answered by Duncan in a brief article, 'Important Hypotheses Reconsidered. VI. Were St. Paul's Imprisonment Epistles written from Ephesus?' (*ET*, lxvii, No. 6 [March 1956], pp. 163-166). Of the Continental scholars, the views of Deissmann are most completely set forth in his essay, 'Zur ephesinischen Gefangenschaft des Apostels Paulus', his contribution to the *Anatolian Studies presented to Sir W. M. Ramsay* (Manchester: M.U.P., 1923); P. Feine, M. Goguel, and W. Michaelis have written extensively on the subject, but their views are most conveniently put before us in their Introductions to the New Testament (see Bibliography III. General). The Ephesian hypothesis is also supported by M. Albertz, most recently in *Die Botschaft des Neuen Testaments*, vol. i, Part II (1952); and by P. Benoît in his remarks on Philippians in *La Bible de Jérusalem* (1953).

It should be remarked that several of the scholars who have accepted the Ephesian origin of Philippians do not, like Duncan, admit it for the other 'imprisonment epistles' (Colossians, Philemon, Ephesians).

(B) *On the Interpretation of ii. (5), 6-11*

All the general treatises on the Christology of the New Testament devote extensive and careful treatment to this hymn, recognizing it to be of cardinal importance for the study of early Christian thought. Among the latest of these may be mentioned:

Cullmann, O., *Die Christologie des Neuen Testaments* (Tübingen: Mohr, 1957); see especially pp. 178-186; 223 f.

Taylor, V., *The Person of Christ in New Testament Teaching* (London: Macmillan, 1958), Part I, chapter 5, 'The Christological "Hymn" in Phil. ii. 6-11'.

All the major commentaries discuss the hymn in extended notes; see especially among the older commentators Vincent, Haupt (with extensive survey of earlier criticism), and Ewald-Wohlenberg; and among the more recent Dibelius and Lohmeyer. But over and above all these discussions which we find incorporated in works of broader scope, there is an apparently endless stream of monographs, essays, and articles bearing upon the literary structure and theological significance of the passage. Since 1927 all criticism has been directed into fresh channels as a result of the investigations of Ernst Lohmeyer, summarized in his commentary on the epistle, but exhibited in detail in his monograph 'Kyrios Jesus. Eine Untersuchung zu Phil. 2. 5-11', published in *Sitzungsberichte der Heidelberger Akademie der Wissenschaften*, Phil.-Hist. Klasse (1928). Its effects will be noted by anyone who compares the second edition of Dibelius' commentary, published in 1925, with his third edition, published in 1937. The following articles represent only a selection from those that have been published in recent years:

Bouyer, L., 'ΑΡΠΑΓΜΟΣ', *RSR*, 39 (1951–1952, *Mélanges Jules Lebreton*), pp. 281-288.

Cerfaux, L., 'L'Hymne au Christ-Serviteur de Dieu (Phil. ii. 6-11 =Is. lii. 13-liii. 12', in *Recueil Lucien Cerfaux: Études d'exégèse et d'histoire religieuse, réunies à l'occasion de son 70ᵉ anniversaire*. 2 vols., Gembloux: Duculot, 1954. (Previously published in the *Miscellanea* presented to A. de Meyer, in 1946.)

Clavier, H., 'Importance du passage christologique au point de vue de la théologie orthodoxe', *Le Christianisme au XXᵉ siècle* (Sept. 5, 1929).

Dupont, J., 'Jésus-Christ dans son abaissement et son exaltation d'après Phil. 2. 6-11', *RSR*, 37 (1950), pp. 500-514.

Feuillet, A., 'L'Homme-Dieu considéré dans sa condition terrestre de 'Serviteur et de Rédempteur (Phil. 2. 5 ss. et textes parallèles)', *RB*, 51 (1942, published under the title *Vivre et penser*, 2ᵉ série), pp. 58-79.

Foerster, W., 'Οὐχ ἁρπαγμὸν ἡγήσατο bei den griechischen Kirchenvätern', *ZNTW*, 29 (1930), pp. 115-128.

Guignebert, C., 'Quelques Remarques d'exégèse sur Phil. 2. 6-11', *RHPR*, 3 (1923), pp. 512-533.

Henry, P., 'Kénose', in *DB Supp*. v, coll. 7-161.

Héring, J., 'Kyrios Anthropos', *RHPR*, 16 (1936), pp. 196-209.

Jeremias, J., 'Zur Gedankenführung in den paulinischen Briefen', 4. 'Christushymnus Phil. 2. 6-11', in *Studia Paulina in honorem J. de Zwaan* (Haarlem: Bohn, 1953), pp. 146-154.

Käsemann, E., 'Kritische Analyse von Phil. 2. 5-11', *ZThK*, 47 (1950), pp. 313-360.

Michel, O., 'Zur Exegese von Phil. 2. 5-11', in *Theologie als Glaubenswagnis*: Festschrift für Karl Heim (Hamburg: Furche, 1954), pp. 79-95.

To these we may add two valuable discussions in treatises on Pauline Christology, viz.:

Andrews, E., *The Meaning of Christ for Paul* (Nashville: Abingdon-Cokesbury, 1955), chap. xi, 'The Pre-existent Christ', especially sec. 2, 'The Incarnation of the Son of God', pp. 154-161.

Porter, F. C., *The Mind of Christ in Paul* (New York & London, Scribner's, 1930), Part IV, 'Christian Thinking about Christ', 3: 'In the form of God', and 4: 'Jesus Christ is Lord', pp. 204-240. These thirty-six pages are given to theological exposition of the hymn.

(C) *On Paul and Stoicism*

In the long essay on 'St. Paul and Seneca' which he included in his commentary on Philippians, Bishop Lightfoot remarked that 'the first impression' made by a chain of parallels to Pauline expressions which he quotes from the Roman Stoic 'is striking. They seem to show a general coincidence in the fundamental principles of theology and the leading maxims in ethics. . . . Nevertheless a nearer examination very materially diminishes the force of this impression' (pp. 288 f.). Others have undertaken the enquiry into the relationship between Paul and the Stoic teachers along other lines. Attention may be drawn to the following:

Bonhöffer, A., *Epiktet und das Neue Testament* (Religionsgeschichtliche Versuche und Vorarbeiten, x). Giessen: Töpelmann, 1910. Teil II, Abschnitt 3, 'Paulus', pp. 98-180.

Enslin, M. S., *The Ethics of Paul* (New York and London: Harper, 1930), Pt. I., 'Forces that Contributed to the Moral Teachings of Paul', chap. ii, 'The Contribution of the Stoa', pp. 17-44.

Festugière, A. J., *L'Idéal religieux des Grecs et l'Évangile.* Paris: Gabalda, 1932. (Études Bibliques.) Excursus D, 'Saint Paul et Marc Aurèle."

Pohlenz, M., 'Paulus und die Stoa', *ZNTW*, 42 (1949), pp. 69-104.

(D) *On the City of Philippi*

Scientific exploration of the site of Philippi began in 1861, under the direction of L. Heuzey of the École Française d'Athènes. All the fundamental studies of the city and the region around it have been published by members of that school. The following may be particularly mentioned:

Heuzey, L., and Daumet, H., *Mission archéologique de la Macédoine.* Paris, 1876.

Perdrizet, P., 'Cultes et mythes du Pangée', in *Annales de l'Est*, xxiv, No. 1, 1910; together with a number of important articles in the *Bulletin de Correspondance Hellénique* from 1894 to 1922.

Picard, C., 'Les Dieux de la colonie de Philippes vers le 1er siècle de notre ère, d'après les ex-voto rupestres', in *RHR*, lxxxvi (1922), pp. 117-201.

Most useful to the general reader, however, are the two comprehensive works of P. Collart and P. Lemerle, viz.:

Collart, P., *Philippes, ville de Macédoine depuis ses origines jusqu'à la fin de l'époque romaine.* 2 vols. Paris, 1937.

Lemerle, P., *Philippes et la Macédoine orientale à l'époque chrétienne et byzantine: Recherches d'histoire et d'archéologie*. Bibliothèque des Écoles Françaises d'Athènes et de Rome, 158. Paris, 1945. Part I, chap. i, 'St. Paul', pp. 7-60.

A brilliant sketch of religious life at Philippi as it would have presented itself to St. Paul is offered by A. J. Festugière in his book *Le Monde gréco-romain au temps de Notre-Seigneur*: II. 'Le Milieu spirituel', pp. 77-83. Paris, 1935.

III. GENERAL

Arndt, W. F., and Gingrich, F. W., *A Greek-English Lexicon of the New Testament and other Early Christian Literature*: a translation and adaptation of the 4th (revised and augmented) edition of W. Bauer's *Griechisch-Deutsches Wörterbuch zu den Schriften des Neuen Testaments und der übrigen urchristlichen Literatur*. Cambridge: C.U.P.; and Chicago: Univ. of Chicago Press, 1957.

Cerfaux, L., *Le Christ dans la théologie de saint Paul*, 2nd ed., Paris: Cerf, 1954.

Cramer, J. A., *Catenae Graecorum Patrum in Novum Testamentum*, Tom. VI. Oxford: O.U.P., 1844.

Davies, W. D., *Paul and Rabbinic Judaism: some Rabbinic Elements in Pauline Theology*, 2nd ed. London: S.P.C.K., 1955.

Feine, P., *Einleitung in das Neue Testament*. 8th ed. rev. J. Behm. Leipzig: Quelle & Meyer, 1936. 11th ed., 1956.

Festugière, A. J., *La Sainteté*. Collection Mythes et Religion, ed. P.-L. Couchoud. Paris: Presses Universitaires, 1942.

Goguel, M., *The Birth of Christianity*, tr. H. C. Snape. London: George Allen & Unwin, 1953.

Goguel, M., *Introduction au Nouveau Testament*. 4 vols. in 5. Paris: Leroux, 1923-1926.

Goguel, M., 'Le Paulinisme: théologie de la liberté', *RThP*, ii (1951), pp. 93-104; iii (1951), pp. 175-183.

Goodspeed, E. J., *An Introduction to the New Testament*. Chicago: Univ. of Chicago Press, 1937.

Goodspeed, E. J., *Problems of New Testament Translation*. Chicago: Univ. of Chicago Press, 1947.

Goodwin, W. W., *Syntax of the Moods and Tenses of the Greek Verb*. Boston: Ginn & Co., 1890.

Gutbrod, W., *Die paulinische Anthropologie*, Beiträge zur Wissenschaft vom Alten und Neuen Testament, hsg. A. Alt und G. Kittel; Vierte Folge, Heft 15. Stuttgart: Kohlhammer, 1934.

Hendry, G. S., *The Gospel of the Incarnation*. Philadelphia: Westminster Press, 1958.

Jackson, F. J. F., and Lake, K., *The Beginnings of Christianity*: Part I, 'The Acts of the Apostles', 5 vols. London: Macmillan, 1920–1933.

Joüon, P., 'Notes philologiques sur quelques versets de l'Épître aux Philippiens', *RSR*, 28 (1938), pp. 89-93, 223-233, 299-310.

Knox, John, *Chapters in a Life of Paul*. Nashville: Abingdon-Cokesbury, 1950.

Knox, John, *Christ the Lord: The Meaning of Jesus in the Early Church*. Chicago: Willett, Clark, 1945.

Knox, W. L., *St. Paul and the Church of the Gentiles*. Cambridge: C.U.P., 1939.

Michaelis, W., *Einleitung in das Neue Testament*, 2nd ed. rev. Bern: Haller, 1954.

Mitton, C. L., *The Epistle to the Ephesians: Its Authorship, Origin and Purpose*. Oxford: Clarendon, 1951. c. xi, 'Comparison between Ephesians and Philippians'; Appendix IV, 'Parallels between Philippians and the other Pauline Epistles'; Appendix V, 'Parallels to Philippians in the other Pauline Epistles'.

Moule, C. F. D., *An Idiom Book of New Testament Greek*. Cambridge: C.U.P., 1953.

Moulton, J. H., and Howard, W. F., *A Grammar of New Testament Greek*, vol. i, 'Prolegomena', 1908; Vol. II, Pt. I, 1919; Pt. II, 1929. Edinburgh: T. & T. Clark.

Moulton, J. H., and Milligan, G., *The Vocabulary of the Greek Testament illustrated from the Papyri and other non-literary Sources*. London: Hodder & Stoughton, 1914–1929.

Nägeli, T., *Der Wortschatz des Apostels Paulus*. Basel, 1904.

Schweitzer, A., *The Mysticism of Paul the Apostle*, tr. W. Montgomery. London: A. & C. Black, 1931.

Schweizer, E., *Erniedrigung und Erhöhung bei Jesus und seinen Nachfolgern*. Zürich: Zwingli-Verlag, 1955. An English version of this important work is announced in the series 'Studies in Biblical Theology', under the title *Humiliation and Exaltation*. Meanwhile a brief account of his thesis is available in his article, 'Discipleship and Belief in Jesus as Lord from Jesus to the Hellenistic Church', tr. H. F. Peacock, in *NTS*, vol. 2, no. 2 (November 1955), pp. 87-99.

Staerk, W., *Soter: die biblische Erlösererwartung als religionsgeschichtliches Problem*. Gütersloh: Bertelsmann, 1933.

Staerk, W., *Soter II: die Erlösererwartung in den östlichen Religionen. Untersuchungen zu den Ausdrucksformen der biblischen Christologie*. 1938.

Zimmerli, W., and Jeremias, *The Servant of the Lord* (tr. from the article παῖς θεοῦ in *ThWB*, v, by H. Knight). Studies in Biblical Theology, 20. London: S.C.M., 1955.

TRANSLATION AND COMMENTARY

THE Greek text which has been used as the basis for the translation and the commentary is the 23rd edition of Dr. Erwin Nestle's *Novum Testamentum Graece*, edited in collaboration with Dr. Kurt Aland (Stuttgart: Bibelanstalt, 1957).

THE EPISTLE TO THE PHILIPPIANS

I.—A LETTER SENT WITH EPAPHRODITUS ON HIS RETURN TO PHILIPPI

(a) INTRODUCTORY SECTION. i. 1-11

I. THE SALUTATION. i. 1-2

(1) Paul and Timothy, slaves of Christ Jesus, to all the saints in Christ Jesus who are in Philippi, with the bishops and deacons: (2) grace to you and peace, from God the Father and the Lord Jesus Christ.

The letters of Paul follow the conventions of Greek usage, with modifications which permit the expression of Christian thoughts and feelings. In contrast with our own practice of naming first the person to whom we are writing, and leaving our own name and the formal expression of our good wishes to the end, the Greek started with the name of the writer, followed by the name of the person addressed, and then the formal greeting: 'X to Y, greetings'. Paul regularly expands all three parts of the opening formula, sometimes working in a statement of the faith which sounds the theme of the epistle, as in Galatians and still more in Romans. It is probable that the unique feature of this salutation, the reference to **bishops and deacons,** if it is not simply an indication that the Roman penchant for organization had already given the Philippian church a regular system of office-bearers, is occasioned by something in the correspondence which has already passed between Paul and the Philippian church. Possibly he wants to bring his commendation of Epaphroditus, who is to carry the letter home with him, to the attention of the leaders,

so that they may see that he is received with the special honour
which Paul bespeaks for him (ii. 29-30).

The two words translated **bishops and deacons** have been
much debated. In the second century they became specialized
in ecclesiastical usage; the bishop as the head of the local
Christian community, the deacons as his assistants in whatever
duties he might assign to them (see B. S. Easton, *The Pastoral
Epistles* [New York: Scribner's, 1947; London: S.C.M. Press],
on 'Bishop', 'Deacon', and 'Ruler', pp. 173-179; 181-185; and
221-228). As long as it was felt that the words must have the
same specialized sense here, some scholars felt bound to hold
that their presence was sufficient of itself to bring the authenticity of the whole epistle into question; others held that these
words must have been interpolated at some later date. It will be
agreed that the words are used as the designation of officers of
the congregation; but there is nothing to indicate the nature of
their offices or functions. Negatively, it may be said that the use
of the plurals rules out any possibility that the Philippian
church is governed by a monarchical bishop. Fifty or sixty
years (possibly even as much as a hundred years) later, Polycarp
of Smyrna speaks of 'presbyters' (or 'elders') and 'deacons'
in the same church, without making any mention of a 'bishop';
it is probable that the 'presbyters' of Polycarp are identical
with the 'bishops' of Paul in the matter of office and function.
In his other letters, Paul seldom mentions officers of the
congregation at all; when he does it is always in functional
terms, as if they bore no established titles (Gal. vi. 6—'he who
teaches'; cf. 1 Thess. v. 12-13 and 1 Cor. xvi. 15 f.; and see my
article, 'The Ministry in the New Testament Church: Practice
and Theory' [*ATR*, xxxvii, No. 1 Jan., 1955], esp. sec. 3, 'The
Ministry as Exercised in the Local Churches', pp. 14-17).
Perhaps the Philippian church had provided itself with a
formal organization more rapidly than other churches; or it may
be that the Apostle makes mention of the local officers here
simply because they have had the chief responsibility for
soliciting and forwarding the gifts which Paul had received.
But it is probably that the words are used non-technically. The
use of our well-established terms **bishops and deacons** is in
fact misleading; the difficulty is to find an adequate rendering

for either of them. *Episcopos* (rendered **bishop**) means 'over-seer', or 'superintendent', in the most mundane contexts; *diakonos* (**deacon**) is the noun cognate with the verb *diakoneo*—'I serve'—and is used in the most down-to-earth way of every kind of service. This passing reference does not provide us with any crumb of information about the status or function of *episcopoi* and *diakonoi* at Philippi; and we are not entitled to read into them in this context the significance which belongs to them in later Catholic usage. There is no reason to think of them as interpolated; it is impossible to imagine circumstances under which such an interpolation would be made in one letter of the Pauline corpus without being extended to the others.

When Paul describes himself and Timothy as **slaves of Christ Jesus,** he is using language which would sound strange and even shocking to Greek ears. Cynics and Stoics would indeed hold that the slave was a man and a brother, and that the wise man is truly free, whatever his civil status; but not even among the philosophers did any Greek speak of his own relation to the divine power which he served as that of a 'slave'. There is no background in Greek usage for the use of **slave** as a figure of religious devotion. Nor did the Hebrew think of himself as a 'slave' of his God. It is strange, therefore, to find that the Greek Old Testament freely employs δοῦλος (**slave**) and its cognates to express the relationship of the true Israelite to his God. Paul is clearly enough making use of a vocabulary created by the Septuagint when he speaks of the Christian life as a 'slavery' to God ('You turned to God from the idols, to be slaves to a God living and true'—1 Thess. i. 9; cf. Rom. vi. 22).

Something more is involved when the Apostle uses the phrase **slaves of Christ Jesus;** there is much boldness in transferring to Jesus the same figure which has been used to express the relationship of the worshipper to God. The Christological implications are obvious. This passionate defender of freedom would not own himself a **slave** except of one to whom he accords divine prerogatives. Yet it is not a mere extension of the O.T. usage. **Slaves** is the correlative of Lord (*kyrios*), the title which he gives to Jesus, which is also used in non-religious language of the *master* of slaves (e.g. Col. iv. 1); by it Paul acknowledges his total submission to the will of Christ, his duty of implicit obedience. It may also be related to the thought that Christ has purchased him at the cost of his own blood; as he appeals to the Corinthians: 'You were bought with a price; then glorify God in your bodies. . . . You were bought with a price; do not be slaves of men' (1 Cor. vi. 20; vii. 23). For 'slavery' to Christ means emancipation from every other form of bondage—from bondage to sin, to uncleanness, to lawlessness (Rom. vi. 19-20), to false gods, to the elemental spirits of the cosmos (Gal. iv. 8-9), or to the Law (Rom. vii. 1-6). It is the **slaves of Christ Jesus,** not the autonomous wise men of Cynic or Stoic ideal, who possess the only true and perfect freedom.

A different interpretation of Paul's use of the term **slaves** is proposed by G. Sass. Through a careful semantic study of the usage of the Hebrew word *'ebed*, which is rendered by δοῦλος in Lxx, he comes to the conclusion that Paul uses the term here as a title of honour (*Ehrentitel*). It 'does not convey the thought of unconditional vassalage and bodily ownership, but the thought that God is acting through this man. Not servitude, but instrumentality stands in the foreground. . . . In one of the latest stages of its development, this term can lose the etymological sense ("slave, possession, servant"), and take on a new, theologically determined significance, in which the emphasis no longer rests on the service, the unfree condition of the man, but wholly upon the work and actions of God with this man. . . . In this sense, δοῦλος remains limited to a few men, entrusted by God with particular tasks in and for the church' ('Zur Bedeutung von δοῦλος bei Paulus', *ZNTW*, 40 [1941], pp. 24-32; this article is a valuable supplement to K. Rengstorf's article in *ThWB*).

The readers are now addressed as **the saints in Christ Jesus.** This is Paul's usual designation for Christians, the rank and file of the members of the church. It does not imply that they are marked by exceptional moral excellence, but that they are set apart for God—'holy' as everything which belongs to the worship of God is holy, even to the vessels and the vestments. They are 'the saints of the Most High' (Dan. vii. 18, 27), who shall receive the kingdom and possess it for ever and ever. The background of the thought is thus eschatological; but their part in the promised kingdom is given to them **in Christ Jesus,** and their holiness derives from their incorporation into him.

2   As in all his greetings, Paul couples **God our Father** and our **Lord Jesus Christ** as together the source of the **grace and peace** which he wishes for his readers. He knows that all the blessings which God has to bestow upon us are to come to us as the gift of the glorified Christ, whom he has exalted.

2. THE THANKSGIVING, WITH THE APOSTLE'S ASSURANCES OF HIS AFFECTION. i. 3-8

(3) I give thanks to my God every time I make mention of you in my prayers, (4) always, in every supplication of mine, making the supplication for all of you with joy, (5) as I think of your fellowship in the furtherance of the gospel from the first day until now, (6) in full confidence that he who began a good work in you will carry it to completion, till the Day of Christ Jesus. (7) It is right that I should have this feeling for you all, because I have you in my heart, for you all share with me in the grace given to me, both in my bonds and in the defence and vindication of the gospel. (8) God is my witness, how I long for you all in the heart of Christ Jesus.

A phrase of thanksgiving at the beginning also belongs to the conventions of Greek letter-writing, and this custom is followed by Paul in every letter except Galatians, where his passionate concern carries him into an immediate expostulation. But his words are no merely conventional expression of thanksgiving. In this letter above all, he is moved by the deepest affection for his readers; it is evident from these first sentences that the Apostle feels a closer sympathy between himself and the Philippians than with any of his other churches. He prays for all his churches, but he could not always say that he was

4 **making the supplication . . . with joy** (e.g. 2 Cor. ii. 1-4). Nor could he feel that other churches had shown the same

5 **fellowship in the furtherance of the gospel** without a break.

He recalls the supplies which they sent to him at Thessalonica
in the early days, which he has mentioned in his letter of thanks
(sent some months earlier, but now incorporated in the latter
part of this letter, iv. 10-20), and their constant helpfulness
since. From other churches, he has been unwilling to accept
even the bare necessities (2 Cor. xi. 8-11), but he has never had
any fear that the Philippians would suspect him of mercenary
designs. They have given ample proof of their loyalty, yet the
Apostle puts his **confidence** for their future steadfastness and **6**
progress not in them, but in God, **who began a good work**
in them and may be trusted to complete it. **The Day of Christ
Jesus** is the day of judgment, the Old Testament 'day of the
Lord'; but while O.T. prophecy tended more and more to
paint that Day in sombre colours ('darkness, and not light; a
day of wrath . . . a day of distress and anguish'—Amos v. 20;
Zeph. i. 15), Christ transforms it for his followers into the day
of salvation; for he 'rescues us from the Wrath to come'
(1 Thess. i. 10; cf. v. 4-10).

The grace given to me is probably to be taken specifically **7**
(as in Rom. i. 5—'grace and apostolic commission'—certainly
to be construed as a *hendiadys*), of the divine **grace** which
enables him in and through his imprisonment (**my bonds**) to
defend and vindicate not alone himself but the gospel which he
preaches. In this grace, the Philippian Christians **all share,**
because they have not been shamed or intimidated by the
imprisonment of their apostolic founder, but have identified
themselves with his cause. Lohmeyer takes the phrase as one of
the indications (which he finds in evidence all through the
epistle) that the Philippian church is at this very time under-
going persecution; but such an interpretation depends upon a
prior acceptance of the notion that the epistle as a whole is a
tractate on martyrdom. The words are simply a grateful recognition that they are with him in spirit, sustaining him by their
sympathy and by their prayers, and sustained themselves by
his cheerful steadfastness; thus they **all share in the grace
given** to Paul for his witness to the gospel. **Defence** and
vindication are technical legal terms; the thought is that in
making his defence, Paul is vindicating the gospel which he
preaches, giving guarantees that it is truly the gospel of God,

entrusted to him for communication to others, and that it
conveys a valid title to the benefits which God has promised.

8   Many interpreters feel that if Paul calls upon God to bear
witness to his longing for them, it can only be because he has
reason to believe that some of them do not feel sure of his
continued affection. Since he shows concern over personal
conflicts within the Philippian church (ii. 2; iv. 2 f.), it is
possible that he wishes to make it perfectly clear that **all** have
the same great place in his heart—indeed, he would say, **in the
heart of Christ Jesus.** His love for them is as wide as his
Master's; it is Christ's love that reaches out to them in Paul.
The frequent repetition of the phrase **you all** through this
section (4, 7, 7b, 8) at least indicates a desire to show that he
makes no distinctions among them, just as he desires that they
show **the same disposition, having the same love, united
in soul, one in disposition** (ii. 2).

3. A PRAYER FOR THE PHILIPPIANS. i. 9-11

**(9) And I pray for this, that your love may more and still
more abound in knowledge and in all perception, (10) so
that you may prove in practice the things that are excellent, that you may be pure and unfaltering against the
Day of Christ, (11) bringing forth a full harvest of righteousness—the harvest which is given through Jesus
Christ, and redounds to the glory and praise of God.**

In the thought of Paul, **love** is the master key to understanding, to the moral and spiritual discrimination which is
developed by practice, and to all the fruits that life may yield
under the touch of Christ.

9   **Your love**—not particularly their love for him, corresponding to the warmth of his affection for them; nor yet their love
for one another, though this is of course included in the thought;
but **love** in the most comprehensive sense as the central
element of the Christian life—God's love imparted to us,
'poured out in our hearts through the Holy Spirit' (Rom. v. 5).

This is the true wealth, of which we can never have enough; he prays that it **may more and still more abound.** The increase of **love** is then related to the development of moral insight—**knowledge and all perception.** They will learn more and more to devote themselves to the highest and worthiest things; as Bengel pointed out, it is not so much a matter of distinguishing right from wrong, as the best among good things (*in bonis optima*). The verb translated **prove in practice** sometimes means 'approve', but there is always in the background the notion of an approval that follows upon testing (Rom. xii. 2 —'prove what is the will of God'). A warm heart is not enough; it needs to learn through experience to direct its impulses into the noblest channels. Paul uses the same phrase in Romans ii. 18, of the mistaken outlook of the Jew who boasts that he 'knows the will of God and approves the things that are excellent', because he is instructed out of the Law. For Paul, this high spiritual perception cannot be taught from any book, not even from the sacred scriptures; it can only be developed through experience in the life of active **love.**

Unfaltering—the word so rendered may mean either 'with- 10 out stumbling', or 'not causing others to stumble': Chrysostom takes it in both senses (cf. Vulg. *sine offensa*, whence AV 'without offence'; but in 1 Cor. x. 32, it clearly means 'giving no offence', i.e. 'putting no stumblingblock in the way'). It is possible that Paul is warning them against misguided zeal, which may cause serious damage even though inspired by the purest affection and unselfishness.

Bringing forth a full harvest—the participle is taken in the 11 middle sense in preference to the passive ('being filled with the fruits of righteousness'). The thought is not that **righteousness** is itself the **harvest,** but that it is the right relationship with God which *produces* the **harvest.** The Christian character developed in all its clearness and purity is the end product of the grace by which we were 'justified' (*BKW*, 'Righteousness', pp. 52-54). This harvest is not our own achievement, as if we were successful exponents of morality, but is **given through Jesus Christ.**

Elsewhere Paul speaks of the 'fruit' of Christian character as produced by the Spirit (Gal. v. 22 f.). The **righteousness** which produces such fruits is of course for the Apostle 'not my own righteousness—that which comes by Law; but that which comes through faith in Christ, the righteousness which comes from God, resting upon faith' (iii. 9, below).

The glory and praise of God is the supreme end of all human action. As the **harvest of righteousness** is **given through Jesus Christ** it cannot give grounds for pride or boasting, as if it redounded to our own glory and praise. **The glory** of God is shown forth by the heavens (Ps. xix. 1) and shines upon us in the face of Christ (2 Cor. iv. 6); it is a wonderful thought that it may be granted to us also to manifest the same glory, in the life of love. **The praise of God** for this work of salvation which he **has begun** and may be trusted to complete in us (v. 6) is rendered not only by us, the recipients of his blessing, but by his whole creation.

(b) A REPORT ON THE APOSTLE'S SITUATION AND PROSPECTS. i. 12-26

4. THE EFFECTS OF HIS IMPRISONMENT ON THE LOCAL CHURCH: NEW VIGOUR AND BOLDNESS. i. 12-17

(12) I want you to know, brethren, that this affair of mine has tended rather to the advance of the Gospel. (13) Thus it has come to be recognized by the whole Praetorian Guard and by all the others that if·I am in fetters, it is because of my activities as a Christian; (14) and most of the brethren in the Lord, gaining confidence through my imprisonment, are daring more and more boldly to preach the Word without fear. (15) Some, it must be said, are prompted by jealousy and contention, but some also by goodwill, in preaching Christ. (16) These are moved by love, knowing that I am posted here for the defence of the Gospel; (17) the others are proclaiming Christ out of partisanship, with unhallowed motives, imagining that they are making my imprisonment galling to me.

It might have been thought that the spectacle of the great Apostle in prison would move the rank and file of Christian believers to tread softly for a time, and to seek to avoid the notice of the authorities, lest they should be compelled to share his captivity. The effect has been just the opposite: they have lost their fears, and are bolder than ever in making the gospel known. Some of them are indeed not actuated by the purest motives; they have been jealous of Paul's growing authority and have redoubled their evangelistic activities as it were to spite him, as if that might cause him chagrin; but some **are moved by love,** and by a true appreciation of his position as Christ's ambassador. Meanwhile the pagans themselves, the soldiers who guard him and all the others with whom he has to do, have come to understand the true cause of his imprisonment. It is not that he is charged with any evil deeds, but that he is 'in Christ'. This is of course Paul's way of putting it, not theirs. He is himself deeply sensible of Christ's continued presence with him in his prison; even while the fetters clatter on his legs, he is 'in Christ'. But he feels that it is all to the good, in the interest of his gospel, that the authorities should have come to recognize that he is not a revolutionary agitator or a vicious man, but is in jail because of his work for Christ. The translation here (v. 13) is perhaps too free, but the paraphrase interprets the thought as accurately as possible.

By the whole Praetorian Guard—literally, 'in the whole 13 praetorium'. The meaning of the phrase cannot be determined with certainty. If the letter was written from Ephesus or Caesarea, the 'praetorium' would most naturally be taken as meaning the residence of the head of the Roman administration —the proconsul of Asia or the procurator of Judaea; at Caesarea, Paul was imprisoned 'in Herod's praetorium' (Acts xxiii. 35). If we hold to the tradition of a Roman provenance, it will probably mean **the Praetorian Guard,** as we have rendered it; and it would not be unthinkable that a detachment of praetorians should be stationed for a time at Ephesus or Caesarea, though the cohorts of this imperial guard were generally posted in Italy and at times concentrated in Rome. The word could also be used of the permanent camp which Tiberius built for them (*castra praetoriana*); and it is not impossible that a visitor from the provinces should use the same word for Nero's great 'palace' (so AV) on the Palatine hill, as he was accustomed to use for the residences of governors. This is the interpretation given by such great Greek commentators as Chrysostom, Theodore of Mopsuestia, and Theodoret. Lightfoot's objection to it, which has seemed conclusive to most modern commentators, is 'that not a single instance of this usage has been produced'; and that the feelings of Roman citizens would have been 'outraged by the adoption of a term which implied that they were under a military despotism' (*St. Paul's Epistle to the Philippians*, p. 98.) But a visitor from the East might perfectly well use a term which was not officially adopted, and he might not be fully aware of the touchiness of the Romans on the point. **All the others** will in any case mean everyone else who is concerned with the disposition of the case againt Paul, hardly 'the city at large' (as Vincent suggests). The words do not suggest that Paul is making converts among the soldiers detailed to hold him under guard, and the lawyers appointed to draw up the case for the prosecution, but only that he has succeeded in making them realize that his only offence is the propagation of the gospel. There is no intimation that this clarification of his position has given him good hopes of acquittal and release. He directs his whole attention not to his own prospects, but to **the advance of the Gospel;** anything which causes the gospel to forge its way onward contents him. He does not shrink from martyrdom; he longs to 'know . . . the fellowship of Christ's sufferings, being made conformable to his death' (iii. 10). But his martyrdom can hardly advance the good cause unless the responsible authorities recognize that they are taking action against him for his fidelity to Christ; if it meant nothing more to them than the end of one more Jewish firebrand, they would not find in it a testimony to Christ.

Similarly, we must reject the suggestion that the new confidence of the brethren derives from the belief that once the facts of the case have been established, the prosecution will not go on with the case; Paul himself will soon be released and no others will be thrown into prison with him. Despite the great names that have lent it their support, this interpretation deprives the words of all their force. People cannot be said to

be **daring more and more boldly to preach the Word,** if in 14
fact there is no longer any need for daring, if there is in fact no
longer any personal risk in preaching to their heart's content.
Nor can the words **through my imprisonment** be taken as if
they meant, 'seeing that my imprisonment is not likely to have
any serious consequences'. The thought is manifestly that his
fortitude has kindled theirs; he has given them an example of
unfaltering courage in the face of danger. It is not suggested
that they have been unduly timid before this; it is rather that
their courage has risen to new heights, when they might have
been intimidated.

Preach the word—with AV, following the Textus Receptus,
which can now appeal to the early testimony of the Beatty
Papyrus, $\mathfrak{P}^{46}$. Most of the other good witnesses add 'of God',
with some variation in the word order. The phrase **in the Lord**
is construed by some interpreters with **confident,** instead of
with **the brethren;** C. F. D. Moule regards this as 'extremely
unlikely' (*Idiom Book*, p. 108).

Most of the brethren share this new boldness; the words
imply that some shrink from the danger involved in preaching
the word. More serious, some of the confident and courageous
ones are moved in part by unworthy motives—**jealousy** 15
and contention, and **partisanship.** It is to be noted that 17
the Apostle does not accuse them of false teaching, or of
preaching a perversion of the gospel; consequently, they cannot
be Judaizers or heretics, as has often been suggested. It is not
the content of their message which is found faulty, but the
whole spirit in which they approach their task. It is hard for us
to reconstruct the situation. If we are at Rome, we may be
hearing of groups which were well established before Paul
arrived, of preachers and teachers who were highly regarded by
the Christians of the city, but who feel that the renown of the
great Apostle has put them in the shade. Now they are resolved
to show that they can be as bold as he, and as successful in
winning converts. Or we may imagine factions such as we know
existed in Corinth (1 Cor. i. 11 ff.), and suppose that the
admirers of some unknown Apollos are jealous for their learned
and eloquent leader. They think that Paul has a similar littleness
of mind, and will be irked by their energetic and successful

evangelism. The spectacle of these divisions and partisan jealousies around him adds urgency to his appeal to the Philippians to **stand firm in one spirit, with one mind striving side by side for the faith of the Gospel** (i. 27). The phrase rendered **with unhallowed motives** means literally 'not holily'; the adverb is often rendered 'chastely', and is generally used of the purity of life and character which belongs to true sanctity (see the discussion of the word 'Hagnos' by A. J. Festugière, in his book *La Sainteté*).

Such factions and jealousies might of course have been encountered in Ephesus or in Caesarea, as they certainly were in Corinth; but Acts gives no hint that the church at Ephesus was not wholly loyal to its great founder, and Caesarea would, we might suppose, be sufficiently in the shadow of the mother church of Jerusalem not to be moved by jealousy of the apostle of the Gentiles. The situation is more easily understood of Rome, which had known no Christian leaders of the first rank before the arrival of Paul.

5. THE APOSTLE'S ATTITUDE AND OUTLOOK.
i. 18-26

(18) What difference does that make? All that matters is that in one way or another, whether in pretence or in truth, Christ is being proclaimed; and in this I rejoice, yes, and shall rejoice. (19) For I know that "this will turn out for my salvation", through your prayers and the rich provision of the Spirit of Jesus Christ, (20) in accordance with my earnest expectation and hope that I shall not be put to shame in any way, but that now as always, in all freedom, Christ will be magnified in my body, whether it be through my life or my death. (21) For to me, to live is Christ and to die is gain. (22) If I am to go on living in the flesh, this will mean that I shall reap the fruit of my toil—I do not know what to choose; (23) I am drawn strongly both ways. I have the longing to move on and to

be with Christ, for that is far and away the better; (24) but that I should remain in the flesh is more needful for your sakes. (25) And I know, I am persuaded of this, that I shall remain and continue in company with you all, to further your progress and joy in the faith, (26) so that you may have in me abundant cause for glorying in Christ Jesus, through my arrival among you again.

Paul will not allow himself to be disturbed by personal 18 hostility to himself, or even by impurity of motives on the part of these zealous preachers. Whatever the spirit in which they go about their work, **whether in pretence or in truth, Christ is being proclaimed;** and so the main end is being served— **the advance of the Gospel** (v. 12). Paul has insisted elsewhere that the power of the gospel does not depend upon the eloquence or dialectical skill with which it is presented (1 Cor. i. 17 f.; ii. 1-5); here he implies that it is not dependent upon the character and disposition of the preacher. There is a certain parallelism here with the church's firm insistence that the validity of the sacraments does not depend upon the personal worthiness of the minister. This is not to say that Paul sets little store by sincerity and purity of heart. He disavows any resort to the tricks of the orator or the cleverness of the sophist to commend his gospel; but he makes it clear that he has 'renounced underhanded, shameful ways, not practising trickery or handling the word of God guilefully, but by the open declaration of the truth commending [himself] to every man's conscience in the sight of God' (2 Cor. iv. 2). Yet he will not suggest that the gospel is emptied of its power by the insincerity of others. **Pretence**—a strange word to use in the context. It can hardly be meant to suggest that these people do not really believe the gospel which they are preaching, but rather that their preaching is a cover for their attacks on Paul; they are more concerned to gall him than to win men for Christ. It is clear enough that Paul is deeply hurt by these antagonisms; he is not thick-skinned, and he has no touch of the arrogance that can shrug off the backbiting of little people with unconcern or disdain. But he is able to rise above his own hurt feelings and to find joy in the vigorous activity of the preachers. There is a high magnanimity in the saying: **Christ is being preached, and in this I rejoice, Yes, and shall rejoice.**

19   **'This will turn out for my salvation.'** Paul is quoting the words of Job as they are rendered in the Septuagint (Job xiii. 16). Paul, like Job, is confident of ultimate vindication by God, despite the hazards of his immediate situation. **Salvation** here must be given its full eschatological sense; it cannot be taken to mean merely 'deliverance' from his present plight. Paul is not confident that he will be freed from his prison, but that he will endure to the end and so be saved in the Day of Christ (Matt. xxiv. 13; Rev. ii. 10; etc.). Yet he knows that if he is to endure, he will need more than his own human strength; he will need to be sustained by the **prayers** of the Philippians and by **the rich provision of the Spirit of Jesus Christ.** The latter phrase may be taken in the sense that the **Spirit** is itself the **rich provision** which he needs; but it is probably better to take it in the sense that **the Spirit** dispenses the **rich provision** of faith and courage which Paul will need, in response to the **prayers** of the church.

20   The only **shame** for Paul would be in a failure to stand firm in loyalty to Christ. Not jail nor even execution will cause him to be ashamed in any way. His one concern is that he may never falter in his testimony to Christ. His **hope** is not that he may show himself a hero under his ordeals, but that whatever comes, **Christ will be magnified.** Paul has given long proof of his fidelity; the phrase **now as always, in all freedom** carries in it the claim that he has been true in every previous crisis. **Freedom**—the word which Paul uses here means primarily 'forthrightness of speech', and then more broadly 'boldness', especially the courage appropriate to the free man, which acts openly even in a hostile atmosphere—the spirit of true **freedom** which no threats can reduce to silence.

Paul contemplates with an equal mind the prospect of death, not because life has lost its delights or has no longer any satisfactions for him, but because death means greater fulness of a
21 life that is already rich and full. **To me to live is Christ,** and so life is filled with heavenly blessings; yet even for such a life— we might better say, especially for such a life—**to die is gain.** There is no thought here that the life of earth is hard, and only to be endured by reason of the prospect of a better life in another

world. Life as Paul knows it—the life which he now lives in the flesh by faith in God and in Christ (Gal. ii. 20)—is good above all things, so good that he can only describe it by saying **to me to live is Christ;** yet even for such a life, precisely for such a life, **to die is gain.**

At this point, the language of St. Paul becomes irregular and broken, reflecting vividly the movements of his thought as he passes swiftly from the plans for renewed labour which form in his mind whenever he entertains the possibility of release from prison, to the almost rapturous contemplation of a death which will mean for him a closer communion with Christ. If there were only his own **desire** to be considered, his choice 23 would be **to move on** (the Greek verb goes back to the nautical metaphor of a ship weighing anchor and putting out to sea) **and to be with Christ.** He piles comparative on comparative as he exclaims (to render literally); 'by far more better'—**far and away the better.** But the choice is not for him to make, and his **desire** is not the ruling principle of his life. He is Christ's slave, and must do Christ's will, and he will accept with a glad heart whatever Christ has in store for him. Indeed, he can see that a renewed period of activity will have rewards of another kind—**fruit of toil.** The phrase may mean 'fruitful toil', or 22 (more probably) it may convey the suggestion that he will be able to **reap the fruit** of **toil** which he has been obliged to leave incomplete, when he was arrested and thrown into jail. And apart from his own satisfactions, he can see that for the sake of the Christians of Philippi, and for the church generally, it **is** 24 **more needful that (he) should remain in the flesh.** Even if the choice were left to him, he would not **know what to** 22 **choose.** But the more his mind dwells on the needs of his churches, and on the help that he could still give them, the more he is convinced that he will **remain** in this life . . . **to** 25 **further (their) progress and joy in the faith.** He will even speak of his **arrival** among them as his *parousia*—the very word 26 which he uses of the 'coming' of the Lord Jesus Christ (1 Thess. iii. 13, and often). The word was used in profane Greek of the ceremonious entry of a king or governor into a city, with all the manifestations of joy which attended it. He knows that he will receive a king's welcome from them when he comes.

ADDITIONAL NOTE.   On Paul's Expectation of the Life to
   Come

**For to me to live is Christ and to die is gain. . . . I have
the longing to move on and to be with Christ, for that is
far and away the better** (verses 21, 23). Unless we are to hold
that Paul's conception of the fulfilment of the Christian's hope
of blessedness had radically changed by the time that he wrote
these words, so that he no longer believed that he would have
his 'perfect consummation and bliss' only at the coming of the
Lord in glory, we can hardly fail to find in this sentence some
intimation of an intermediate state. Fr. L. S. Thornton, after
citing verses 21 and 23, goes on to say: 'This utterance stands
out as a classic statement of faith with regard to the Christian
attitude towards death. It consists of two sentences, in each of
which death seems to be regarded as the gateway into a fuller
form of the life in Christ. . . . Moreover, it is clear that the
Apostle is not here thinking of a distant heavenly bliss beyond
the intermediate state. He is speaking of a condition which
follows immediately upon death.

'It does not follow, however, that this statement excludes
the notion of an intermediate state. For in an earlier epistle he
makes it clear that our filial relation to God in Christ is to be
fully attained only in "the redemption of the body" (Rom. 8.
23). . . . It would appear, then, that death is not the end of our
pilgrimage, but rather the gateway into a more advanced stage
of that pilgrimage wherein some grave hindrances which at
present hamper us have been removed. As to the details
scripture maintains a wholesome reserve.' He goes on to argue
that we must not suppose that we are not entitled to generalize
from the case of one so pre-eminent as St. Paul; and proceeds:
'If then we may regard his statement (that the life beyond death
is "very far better" precisely because it is a being "with Christ")
as typical, there is one further conclusion to be drawn from it.
If it places the departed souls in a position of advantage over
those Christians who are still living the earthly life, it also, and
with equal emphasis, indicates a continuity of pattern, in that
both stages of the Christian pilgrimage are centred in Christ.'
And again, after speaking of the parallel that may be drawn

'between the saving death of Jesus and every holy Christian death', he proceeds: 'In such a parallel, however, there is not only likeness but also inevitable contrast. Our Saviour's pilgrimage ended with the death which constituted final victory; ours continues through a period of waiting. Yet, although they still wait for heavenly bliss, the departed souls have been released from "the body of sin", and therefore they may, and surely do, anticipate in some degree the consummation of their hope in Christ' (*Christ and the Church* [London: Dacre Press, 1956], pp. 137-140; the whole chapter, on 'The Resurrection of Man', should be read). Dr. Thornton undoubtedly goes beyond the letter of the text, but some development of thought along similar lines is surely required, if we are to give due weight to the overwhelming importance which Paul attaches to the transformation which the Saviour is to effect in us at his Coming from heaven, when he 'will refashion our body of lowliness to share the form of his body of glory' (iii. 21). See the further discussion in the notes on the latter passage.

It might be remarked that a radical Protestant like Oscar Cullmann is if anything even firmer than Fr. Thornton in his insistence that Paul, and the whole New Testament with him, teaches that the Christian does not enter into the state of his final perfection at death; though he does not use the phrase 'intermediate state', his interpretation quite definitely presents the idea. Thus he can write: 'Our bodies will not rise immediately after death, but only at the end of time. This is the general expectation of the New Testament which, in this respect, differs not only from the Greek belief in the immortality of the soul, but also from the view that the dead live even before the *parousia* beyond time, and thus at once enjoy the fruits of the final fulfilment' ('The Proleptic Deliverance of the Body according to the New Testament', in *The Early Church*, ed. A. J. B. Higgins, London: S.C.M., 1956, Essay VIII, pp. 165 ff.). This is in sharp conflict with the position taken by Albert Schweitzer (*The Mysticism of Paul the Apostle* [London: A. & C. Black, 1931], pp. 90 ff., 109 ff.).

(c) EXHORTATIONS TO UNITY. i. 27-ii. 18

6. FIRST EXHORTATION: AN APPEAL FOR UNITY AND FEARLESSNESS IN THE FACE OF THE ENEMIES OF THE GOSPEL. i. 27-30

(27) Only, let your life be ordered in a manner worthy of Christ's gospel, so that whether I come and see you for myself, or in my absence hear about your doings from others, I may learn that you are standing firm—in one spirit, with one mind striving side by side for the faith of the gospel (28) and never being scared in any way by those who are opposed to you. To them, this is a manifest token of (their own) perdition, and of your salvation—a token given by God. (29) For to you it is granted for Christ's sake, not only to believe in him, but also to suffer for him; (30) for you are carrying on the same contest as that in which I am engaged, as you once saw and now hear about me.

27   **Let your life be ordered**—renders the unusual verb πολιτεύεσθαι, which occurs only twice in the New Testament; it is cognate with the noun *politeuma* ('Commonwealth', or 'citizenship') of iii. 21. Both are formed upon the stem of the word *polis*, which to the Greek meant both 'city' and 'state', and is the root of our words 'polity', 'politics', and so forth. The *polis* of ancient Greece was not merely a place of human habitation, but was the theatre of corporate activity of every kind, in which the individual citizen found scope for the use of all his gifts and the realization of all his potentialities; it was 'the highest of all fellowships or associations, which embraces all the others and exists for the attainment of the highest of all goods' (Aristotle, *Politics*, A. 1252 a). The verb as used here by Paul rests upon the transfer of these general conceptions to the church, and bears upon the *corporate* life of the Christian community of Philippi. The Apostle speaks of 'political' activity, not in the ordinary sense, of course, but in the transferred sense of common action in the sphere of the new heaven-

centred *politeuma* of faith, love, and hope. In an earthly state, the aims and ideals are largely the product of its historical and cultural achievement, and men strive to be worthy of those who made their city great. In the Christian community, the determining factor of life is the gospel, and men are challenged to live **in a manner worthy of Christ's gospel.**

But this community is engaged in a life-and-death conflict, and the worthiness to which it is called consists in firmness, unity, and dauntless courage. Paul wants to learn that they are **standing firm,** like an army resolute to repulse the fiercest attacks. His metaphor shifts quickly to the picture of a team of athletes, united in mind and spirit. **With one mind**—literally, 'in one soul'. There is no need here to go carefully into Paul's distinction of 'soul' and 'spirit'; the double phrase simply lends emphasis to the demand for entire inward unity. The spectacle of the competing groups around him in the Roman church (or the Ephesian, if you will); with their fierce partisanship and petty jealousies, adds urgency to his appeal that the Philippians may not allow their common effort to be weakened by divisions among themselves. **Scared**—again a rare word in 28 Greek, sometimes used of the shying of a startled horse. The phrase suggests that the opponents of the Christians tried to strike terror into their hearts, to throw them into a panic.

The steadfastness of the Christians, their firmness and unity in the face of all attempts to frighten them, will be to their opponents **a manifest token of perdition, and of your salvation.** The Greek text has a certain lack of balance here, and this has led to a number of variants which have been introduced in the attempt to establish a clear antithesis. In particular, the possessive pronoun has been changed from the genitive (ὑμῶν) to the dative (ὑμῖν); to give the sense: 'to them, a token of perdition; to you, a token of salvation'. It is recognized by all critics that the genitive is the true reading; but it is surprising to find that a large number of commentators continue to interpret the clause as if the dative were read. The antithesis, however, is not made between 'them' and 'you'; but between **perdition** and **salvation;** the true balance of the clauses is therefore that which is indicated in the translation: **To them . . . a manifest token of (their own) perdition and of your**

salvation. The thought is not that the steadfastness of the Christians has one meaning for their opponents and another for themselves; it is a token *to their opponents*—a double token; it imposes upon them the unwelcome conviction that they are storing up tribulation and anguish for themselves against the day of judgment, and that the Christians whom they are persecuting have God on their side and are assured of **salvation.** And this double token is **a token given by God.** The Apostle suggests that God is working secretly upon the minds and consciences of the persecutors, with premonitions of their own doom and persuasions of the good that awaits the persecuted. May we not perceive here Paul's recollection of his own inward experience as a persecutor, when he found himself 'kicking against the goad' (Acts ix. 5, Vulgate)? Or is it, as Haupt suggests, that beneath all the fury of his own opponents he had divined 'the feeling of an inward brokenness and an inner discomfiture despite the seeming triumph'? **Perdition** and **salvation** both refer to the final destiny of men as it will be appointed to them in the day of judgment; they have no reference to the earthly issue of the persecutions.

29   **Granted**—the Greek verb ($\dot{\epsilon}\chi\alpha\rho\dot{\iota}\sigma\theta\eta$) is formed upon the stem of the noun $\chi\acute{\alpha}\rho\iota\varsigma$, 'grace'. If they suffer, it is not that God has forsaken them or turned his face from them. **To suffer for his sake** is a mark of his signal favour, a grace **granted** for Christ's sake. So we are told that the Apostles Peter and John 'went out from the presence of the Sanhedrin rejoicing, because they had been counted worthy to suffer shame for the Name' (Acts v. 41—they had just been flogged). And Paul himself, as we shall see, is prepared to sacrifice everything that he has ever prized, that he may win Christ: **to know him and the power of his resurrection and fellowship of his sufferings** (Phil. iii. 8-10).

30   **Contest**—the Greek word is commonly used of the great athletic competitions which were a feature of ancient religion, such as the Olympic games. Paul is picturing the Christians as athletes in the arena, engaged in a wrestling match. In one sense, their opponents are the pagans who persecute them and try to force them to renounce Christ. But deeper than this is the thought that 'our wrestling is not against blood and flesh,

but against . . . the world-rulers of this dark age, against the spiritual powers of evil in the heavenly places' (Eph. vi. 12). Thus the Apostle can think of all Christians everywhere as **carrying on the same contest;** he himself at Rome and his friends at Philippi are engaged in a common struggle, which is also part and parcel of the conflict in which they had seen him engaged at Philippi in the early days, against the demonic powers that are vainly striving to overthrow the church of God and the gospel. The participle συναθλοῦντες—**striving together** (v. 27) belongs to the same imagery.

CHAPTER TWO

7. SECOND EXHORTATION: THE APPEAL FOR
   UNITY IN THE COMMON LIFE, GROUNDED
   IN SELF-ABNEGATION AND CONCERN FOR
   OTHERS. ii. 1-4

**(1) If there be then any exhortation in Christ, if there be
any consolation of love, if there be any fellowship of the
Spirit, if there be any tenderness and pity, (2) bring my
joy to the full by showing the same disposition, having
the same love, united in soul, one in disposition; (3)
never moved by partisanship or by vain ambition, but
in humility counting others better than yourselves; (4)
each considering not his own rights but also the rights
of others.**

This painfully literal rendering is given at this point to avoid
imposing a particular interpretation where many details are in
dispute.

1   Paul now appears to be casting around for any and every
kind of thought, feeling, and Christian experience to which he
may appeal, that may move them to respond to his plea for
unity. In the preceding section, he has urged them to present a
united front to the world, to stand shoulder to shoulder against
their pagan foes. Now he pleads with still greater earnestness
for unity within the fold, for concord of spirit within the
Christian community itself. The 'if' clauses of the first verse
contain no verb in Greek, and our first problem is to determine
what verb is to be understood. In our very literal rendering
above we have supplied the verb 'be', as in AV and in most
modern translations. But there is perhaps more to be said for
something with the sense of 'avail', or 'have power'. We might
then paraphrase, 'If an exhortation in Christ has any power to
move you'. The Apostle speaks of an **exhortation in Christ,**

because he wants to emphasize that this is no merely personal plea. He and they are alike **in Christ,** members of his church, sharers in his life; and he speaks to them within that sphere of grace to which they have access through Christ (Rom. v. 2).

Consolation of love, in this context, will then most naturally be taken as an appeal to their experience of the **consolation** which Christ's **love** for them has brought to them in their dangers and sufferings; though there may be a secondary thought of the mutual love which binds together the Apostle and the Christian believers of Philippi. **Fellowship** (or 'communion') **of the Spirit** is another appeal to the realities of Christian experience. *Koinonia* **(fellowship)** is at once participation in the Spirit, enjoying a share of the divine Spirit which is given in measure to every believer; and the common life created by the Spirit and determined in all its motions by the Spirit, which informs the Christian society and makes it a true community. The Spirit of God, which is at the same time the Spirit of Christ (cf. Rom. viii. 9 f.), brings the Christians of Philippi together in the unity of a spiritual life, in which the Apostle also shares.

In strict consistency, the fourth clause also would be taken as an appeal to their experience of the **tenderness and pity** of Christ, his merciful goodness to them. Literally, the expression is 'bowels' (or in our idiom better, 'heart', as the seat of affection; cf. i. 8—**I long for you all in the heart of Christ Jesus**) 'and mercies'; the latter word is used concretely by Paul in Romans xii. 1 ('the mercies of God') of God's merciful acts in Christ, which should move us to entire dedication of ourselves to Him. The sense would then be: 'If Christ in his mercy has redeemed you'. But we must not be too rigorous; and indeed this thought passes over readily enough to that of the tenderness and pity which have been stirred in their hearts through the grace of Christ. The appeal may then be taken in the sense: 'If you have any tenderness and pity in your hearts'. We might then paraphrase the Apostle's plea to this effect: 'If the exhortation of a Christian brother to his Christian brethren has any power to move you; if you remember the consolation which the love of Christ affords; if you are linked with me in the fellowship of the common life which the Holy Spirit creates and

sustains;—or indeed if there is any tenderness, any pity in your
hearts (as I know there is), then fill my cup of joy to the full by
forgetting all your quarrels and jealousies and selfish pride, and
living and working in a complete concord of hearts and minds'.
It is clear that these 'if' clauses are not truly conditional, but
are appeals to presupposed realities. The construction (without
verb) and the sense given are classical; cf. Plato, *Phaedrus*
260 D: 'If my advice [counts for] anything' (with the clear
assumption that it does in fact carry weight).

2   The Apostle takes great **joy** in the Philippian church; not
only does he tell them so directly (i. 4; iv. 1), but the glad note
sounds its music all through the epistle. Only one thing is
lacking to make his joy complete—that perfect harmony should
reign among them. He is distressed to hear that they are not
wholly of one mind. It is evident that the division is over
personal rivalries, not over moral problems or doctrine. He has
no need to rebuke errors; he can only appeal for the putting
aside of personal claims. As in verse 1 he has multiplied the
grounds of his appeal, so now he multiplies the forms in which
he voices it. Chrysostom exclaims with astonishment: '*Babai!*
How often he says "the same", with great insistence!' All the
phrases are, strictly speaking, untranslatable. The verb φρονέω
(twice in v. 2, again in v. 5; twice in iii. 15), means 'to think, to
be minded', but not primarily in an intellectual sense; it bears
rather upon the entire orientation of the emotions and the will
—the whole inward **disposition. The same love**—that is,
the love which gives and is given, mutual love. The last two
phrases are to be taken closely together (H. A. W. Meyer):
the fellowship of souls affords the basis for the unity of
sentiments.

3   It is not unlikely that the lamentable spectacle of groups
divided by partisan rivalries in the city of his imprisonment
moves the Apostle to warn his readers against **partisanship**
and **vain ambition;** he sees the germ of greater troubles in the
personal conflicts which mar the unity of the Philippian church.
Instead of seeking a personal pre-eminence, the empty glory to
which ambition prompts us, we are taught to be rivals only in
the height of the esteem we accord to others.

4   **His own rights . . . the rights of others.** The Greek phrase

is not so definite: it is as vague as the 'things' of AV. So far as the words go, the meaning could be: 'Let not everyone keep a sharp watch over his own possessions, but let each watch over the possessions of others as well'. But this is hardly compatible with the context. The choice really lies between **rights** and 'qualities', or 'gifts'. The underlying situation seems to be one in which individuals are claiming high position for themselves in the church as a matter of right; probably a right based on the spiritual gifts which each possesses. 1 Corinthians xii is directed towards a similar situation; there Paul seeks to make it clear that the different gifts are all to be valued, and used for the edification of the entire community under a deep sense of mutual obligation and mutual need. In the fellowship of the church of Christ, there must be no thought that exceptional gifts confer **rights** to special honours. We are in any case not to insist on our own **rights** (cf. 1 Cor. vi. 7—'Why do you not rather accept unfair treatment? Why are you not rather defrauded?'). If we were all more eager to see that others received all due honour than to claim what we feel to be our own due, there would be little place for disputes and rivalries. Paul does not suggest that anyone is claiming for himself honours that are undeserved; the point is precisely that we must not insist on receiving even the honours that we entirely deserve. For the law of the Christian life is renunciation, not self-assertion; concern for others, not concern for ourselves and our precious **rights.**

8. A HYMN TO CHRIST, HUMILIATED AND GLORI-FIED, THE LORD OF ALL CREATION. ii. 5-11

(5) Let this be the disposition that governs in your common life, as is fitting in Christ Jesus. (6) For he

(First Strophe)
> **Being in the form of God,**
> **Counted not as plunder**
> **Equality with God,**

(7) But stripped himself
    By taking the form of a slave,
    Being made in the likeness of men;

(8) And being found in shape as a man,
    He humbled himself
    In becoming obedient unto death
    (and that, death on a cross).

(Second Strophe)

(9) Therefore God also exalted him to
        the highest station
    And conferred upon him the Name
    That is above every Name,

(10) That in the Name of Jesus
     Every knee should bow
     Of dwellers in heaven, and on earth,
        and in the underworld,

(11) And that every tongue should acclaim him:
     'Jesus Christ is Lord'—
     To the glory of God the Father.

Few passages in the New Testament have been the object of such intensive study as this little hymn—perhaps none except the Sermon on the Mount; and few have given rise to such a diversity of interpretations. Since 1927, study has been directed into new channels through the work of Ernst Lohmeyer, first in his dissertation *Kyrios Jesus* and then in his commentary on the epistle. The interpretation which is here offered is largely indebted to these writings, and to the penetrating and weighty 'Kritische Analyse' of Ernst Käsemann (see the special section of the bibliography bearing upon the passage). Lohmeyer's analysis of the structure of the hymn, which is reflected in the translation given above, is wholly convincing (though a different arrangement is preferred by M. Dibelius and others). It consists of two strophes, each of three stanzas, each stanza in three lines. It is not a fragment, but a totality, a self-contained Hymn which recites the Descent of the Redeemer from heaven to the world of men and to the realm of the dead (the threefold universe); and his Ascent to heaven as Victor, enthroned in glory by God, to whom he has given complete obedience, and receiving the homage of the threefold universe in the acclamations of the mighty spirit-rulers of these realms which he has subdued. This is the Story of Salvation, told in the form of the myth of the Heavenly Redeemer (probably of Iranian origin) who descends from heaven that he may again ascend into heaven, laden with the trophies of victory and opening the way for his followers. The mythological construction is kept but the divine Hero of the myth is identified with Jesus; it is brought into effective relation with the concrete historical person of the Saviour. (Clearly, the passage raises for us in the most acute way the whole problem of 'Kerygma and Myth', the whole difficult question of 'Demythologising'.) But if the passage is thus understood, it is manifestly wrong to think of it in terms of the presentation of Christ as the ethical ideal for our imitation. The hymn belongs in the realm of soteriology, not of Christology or of ethics. Unquestionably, it is made *in its entirety* the ground of the ethical appeal; what is put forward as the ground is not the human personality of Jesus (this is not even in the mind of the author of the hymn or of Paul, who uses it), but the gospel story itself, the fact of the redemptive victory which Christ has won.

This—the whole **disposition** described in verses 2 to 4. The 5 relative clause again lacks a verb. It is certainly wrong to supply the verb 'was' (as in AV—'Let this mind be in you, which was also in Christ Jesus'); such a rendering is impossible in itself, and leads to a total misunderstanding of the sense of the whole passage.[1] **This** is retrospective; and **in Christ Jesus** bears upon the condition, the sphere, the *locus* of the Christian life, not upon the inward disposition of Jesus. The Christians of Philippi, like all Christians, are **in Christ Jesus,** incorporated into him as members of his body, as branches in the Vine (John xv). **In your common life** of the first clause is a parallel expression (literally 'in you'), and will mean not 'in your inmost selves', but 'in your community (of faith and love)'. The parallelism of expression must be allowed to determine the

_____
[1] It is partly occasioned by the inferior reading φρονείσθω of the Textus Receptus.

verb that is to be supplied in the second clause; it must be the same verb as in the first clause: 'the **disposition** which you have, or which alone **is fitting,** as men who are **in Christ Jesus**'. Their mutual relations within the Christian community are to be analogous with the relations of the Christian with Christ. The whole atmosphere and attitude of life in the Christian community must always be that which befits those who are **in Christ Jesus;** and that is the likemindedness, the unity of soul, the humility, the mutual esteem and mutual concern which has been enjoined in verses 2-4.

The hymn which follows (vv. 6 to 11) is not a description of the moral disposition of our Lord, but an elevated recital of his saving *acts.* It is to be noted that all the verbs are *aorists,* 'expressing only the occurrence of an action or the entrance into a state or condition' (W. W. Goodwin, *Syntax of the Moods and Tenses of the Greek Verb,* 56; and see the remarks on the aorist in J. H. Moulton, *Grammar of New Testament Greek,* vol. i, 'Prolegomena', chap. vi, 'The Verb: Tenses and Modes of Action'). All the participles are likewise aorists, except the first (ὑπάρχων . . . **being**). The vocabulary is not to be taken as the technical terminology of a philosophical (or theological) system, least of all is it to be accorded the fixity of any classical system. Nor is there any good reason to hold that the hymn is a translation from Aramaic (as does Lohmeyer), and to seek to throw light on its meaning through the reconstruction of the hypothetical Aramaic expressions. Lohmeyer, for instance, discovers 'the Son of Man' in the passage 8 by persuading himself that the phrase **as a man** represents a Greek rendering of the Aramaic phrase *k'bar-nasha* 'as Son of Man'; the necessity of such an hypothesis is by no means demonstrated.[1] As E. Käsemann has shown, the terminology is best interpreted within the frame of Hellenistic (syncretistic) religious thought. P. Bonnard thinks of a possible 'Judaeo-Gnostic' circle as the source of the hymn; but though it is

---

[1] Cf. the remarks of Dom Dupont ('Jésus-Christ dans son abaissement et son exaltation'): 'In this passage, an allusion to the "Son of Man" runs quite as opposite to the intention of St. Paul as an allusion to the "Servant of the Lord". The Apostle is laying his emphasis on the abasement, the emptying and the humiliation of Christ—it was not the moment for giving Him titles of honour.' (P. 508 n.)

difficult to set limits to what might be found in heterodox
Judaism of the Diaspora, which seems to have entered into
multiform combinations with pagan cults and theosophies
(C. Guignebert, *The Jewish World in the Time of Jesus*, trans.
S. H. Hooke [London: Routledge & Kegan Paul, 2nd imp.,
1951], pp. 238-246), it must be said that there is nothing
specifically Jewish about this language. The 'form of God',
and the thought of 'equality with God' are hardly compatible
with any late form of Judaism.[1] The whole tone is peculiarly
and distinctively *Christian*, and Christian against a Hellenistic,
non-Jewish background.

It is scarcely possible that Paul himself composed the hymn,
though E. F. Scott would attribute it to him; and Dibelius and
Michaelis leave the question open. Neither the vocabulary nor
the central emphasis is Pauline. The key words, several of them
at least, have no real parallel in Pauline usage; and it is important
to notice that the second strophe speaks not of Christ's Resurrection, but of his Exaltation. The Resurrection, certainly the
keystone of Paul's doctrine of Christ's triumph, is silently
subsumed under the thought of the Ascension. Most significant
of all, many will feel, is the fact that the mention of the Cross is
so clearly secondary, a gloss which brings a distinctive Pauline
touch somewhat incongruously into a passage in which the
particular form of the death is not significant. For Paul himself
it is not only 'Christ Jesus who died, rather, who was raised
from the dead' (Rom. viii. 34), but 'Christ and him *crucified*'
who is the theme of the gospel, 'God's Wisdom and God's
Power' (1 Cor. i. 23-24; cf. ii. 2). The phrase stands outside
the rhythmic structure of the hymn, and bears all the marks of
a note added by Paul to a hymn which he felt needed this
remembrance of the Cross.

Can we then rightly speak of the hymn as 'pre-Pauline' and
use it as evidence for an earlier stage of Christian thought about
Christ? If Paul is not himself the author, it is clearly earlier than

[1] The feeling of a Jew, even a hellenized Jew of the Diaspora, is seen in
the words of Philo: 'The mind which imagines itself equal to God is a lover
of self and godless'—*Leg. All.* 1. 49. See also the careful remarks of C. H.
Dodd on the Jewish charge that Jesus, in calling God His own Father, was
making Himself 'equal to God'—*Interpretation of the Fourth Gospel* (Cambridge: C.U.P., 1953), pp. 325 ff.

the epistle to the Philippians; but we must insist that this
affords no justification for assuming that it reflects the thought
of a pre-Pauline Gentile Christianity, or even of a Gentile
Christianity independent of Paul. We know nothing of the
origin of the hymn. If the Apostle uses it, it is not unlikely that
it was first composed by a gifted writer of his own circle, who
had learned from him to think of Christ as 'the Man from
Heaven' (1 Cor. xv. 47), who 'being rich, impoverished himself for your sakes' (2 Cor. viii. 9). The hymn is substantially an
elaboration of these two unquestionably Pauline phrases, given
mythological expression in terms derived from a variety of
sources (partly Old Testament, partly it may be an Iranian [?]
redemption-myth of the Descent of the Redeemer). He is
faithful to Paul's thought also in speaking of God as the subject
and Christ as the object all through the second strophe. It is
God who exalts Christ, as in Paul's own language it is God who
raises Christ from the dead; and the Exaltation of Christ and
the acclamation which he receives from the universe redound
to **the glory of God the Father.** What we have before us,
then, seems to be not a 'pre-Pauline' hymn, but a hymn
composed in Pauline circles, under Pauline influence, but
introducing certain themes into the proclamation of Christ's
victory which are elaborated independently of Paul.

6-8   *First Strophe.* The first strophe of the hymn speaks of
Christ's pre-existent condition in divine **form** (v. 6), of his
incarnation (v. 7), and of his humiliation, expressed in an
obedience extending to the acceptance of **death** (v. 8). Existing
in heaven, he voluntarily submits to the conditions of human
life upon earth **(the form of a slave),** and in the fullness of
obedience even enters the realm of **death.**

Many of the questions which are raised by these words in the
mind of the theologian cannot receive an answer from within
the hymn itself, because they are questions which are not
present in the mind of the author. The relationship between
Christ and God is not precisely defined. **Form** (*morphē*) is not
a synonym for 'substance' (*ousia*); the ontological concern of
later dogmatic theology is not relevant here. **Being in the
form of God** is not equivalent to 'being God', any more than
the form of a slave involves the notion that Jesus was in the

ground of his being **a slave**. Both phrases speak of the condition
of his existence, in heaven and on earth respectively. Yet
morphē **(form)** does, or at least can, retain in the usage of the
New Testament its proper sense of 'form which corresponds
to the underlying reality', in contrast with *schēma* (**shape,** or 8a
'fashion'—AV) which may mean 'a false appearance'. In the
corresponding verbs, for instance, Jesus is 'transformed' or
'transfigured' (verb from the root *morph-*) when he is manifested to his disciples in glorious splendour; that is the true
form of his being (Mark ix. 2 and parallels). But when Satan
is 'transformed' into an angel of light, and his servants into
servants of righteousness (2 Cor. xi. 14), the verb used is a
compound of *schēma*, for this transformation is a disguise, a
masquerade. Similarly, Christian believers are being *meta-
morphosed* into the image of Christ (2 Cor. iii. 18), for this is the
true form of their new life; but they are exhorted not to be
'conformed in fashion to this world' (Rom. xii. 2—another
verb compounded with the root *schēma*); because the 'fashion
of this world' would disguise their true nature. **The form of
God** is therefore not to be conceived as a mere appearance, but
as a form of existence which in some sense exhibits Christ's
true nature. We may with some reserves adopt the words of
C. A. Anderson Scott: 'In every recognizable aspect of his
personality he was from the beginning Divine' (*Christianity
according to St. Paul* [Cambridge: C.U.P., 1927], p. 36; we are
inclined to hesitate over the word 'personality', which is carried
back from his interpretation of the parallel phrase **the form of
a slave**—'in every recognizable aspect of his personality he
was a thrall').

Plunder—the sense in which we take this word will be
dependent upon the way in which we take the following
equality with God (literally, 'the being on an equality with
God'). Is this phrase virtually synonymous with **being in the
form of God,** or does it suggest a yet higher dignity? Is the
thought that **equality with God** was a prize for which an
unholy ambition might grasp with a robber's greed? In this
line of interpretation, the fact that Christ did not thus grasp at
the highest dignity suggests a contrast with the pride of Lucifer,
who said: 'I will ascend into heaven, I will exalt my throne

above the stars of God . . . I will be like the most High' (Isa. xiv. 13 f.); or with the first Adam who succumbed to the tempter's promise: 'Ye shall be as gods' (Gen. iii. 5). Some such contrast is undoubtedly implied; Adam and Lucifer reached out for divine prerogatives in pride and greed; yet it does not follow that for Christ also **equality with God** could have been viewed as a higher dignity to which it would be impious to aspire. Nothing could be higher than **being in the form of God.** Christ was already in possession of the divine estate to which Lucifer and Adam vainly aspired. **Counted not as plunder,** then, must have the sense that Christ, being in assured possession of divine dignities, did not think of his high estate as a kind of booty which might be his for the seizing.

In these phrases, we hear echoes of Hellenistic 'divine-hero' myths of apotheosis (though this is not to say that there is any direct or conscious dependence of the Christian hymn upon a pagan myth). In the pseudo-Platonic *Axiochus* (364 A), it is said of Herakles that 'he was honoured on an equality with the gods' (ἴσα θεοῖς). And there is a passage in Plutarch's *Fortune or Virtue of Alexander*, 1. 8 (*Moralia*, vol. iv [Loeb Library], 330 D) which has been brought into comparison with our passage by several critics: 'He did not overrun Asia like a brigand, nor did he form the design of rending and ravaging it as a brigand's plunder and the spoils obtained by luck (like Hannibal and others); but wishing to make . . . all mankind a single people, he so fashioned himself' (ἑαυτὸν ἐσχημάτισεν— in the context, however, the verb seems to refer to Alexander's adoption of Asiatic *dress*). See further the article 'Jesus Christ and Alexander the Great', by A. A. T. Ehrhardt (*JTS*, xlvi [1945], pp. 45 f.), and that of W. L. Knox, 'The "Divine Hero" Christology in the New Testament,' (*HTR*, xli [1948], no. 4, pp. 229-249). Knox probably assesses the situation fairly when he remarks that Paul 'had in fact described Jesus in terms which represented Him in very much the same light as some of the most popular cult-figures of the hellenistic world' (p. 231), and that the 'language . . . shows a close affinity with the descriptions and panegyrics of these figures of the pagan world, of whom Herakles was the most prominent. . . . In spite of all condemnations of pagan mythology we find an affinity between Jewish-Christian and pagan language which can hardly be due to chance' (p. 233). Knox does not postulate any direct dependence, but suggests that: 'All that we have is the use of a common stock of ideas, ultimately religious, but adopted by rhetoric and popular philosophy, and carried over into the liturgical and homiletic language of the hellenistic world, including that of the Church' (p. 242). It is not unlikely that the Pauline circle would include some to whom this stock of Hellenistic phrases and ideas would be more familiar than to him, but in adopting this hymn into his correspondence he shows himself willing to follow along this road.

See also the monograph of Marcel Simon, *Hercule et le christianisme* (Paris: Belles-Lettres, 1955), especially chapter iii, 'Théologie héracléenne et christologie', pp. 77-118.

It may be added that the Greek commentators consistently take the phrases **form of God** and **equality with God** as equivalent.

Stripped himself—the verb is κενόω (kenoō), meaning 7 literally 'make empty', whence the term *Kenosis*, and the shaky 'Kenotic' doctrine of the Incarnation (see the Appended Note by Professor E. R. Fairweather). Elsewhere in the New Testament, the verb and its cognates have a uniformly bad sense. The adjective means 'empty-handed', 'vain', 'useless'; and the verb, 'to empty of significance', 'to make worthless or vain' (Rom. iv. 14: 1 Cor. i. 17; etc.). Here the sense is equivalent to the 'beggared himself', 'became as poor as a beggar' of 2 Cor. viii. 9. He lays aside the insignia of majesty and glory.

ADDITIONAL NOTE: On 'Kenosis' as a Moral Ideal.

It is interesting to observe that 'kenosis' or 'kenoticism' is used in an entirely different area of thought, in the vocabulary of 'spirituality', particularly in the Russian church. Long before the 'Kenotic' doctrine of the Incarnation began to cast its spell over Western theologians, the conception of a Christ who abandoned all the glories that he might rightfully have claimed to identify himself in voluntary self-abasement with the lowliness of our humanity was exercising a strange dominion over the Russian imagination. Without seeking to frame any theory of the Incarnation, the Russian saints held forth as the ideal of the Christian life the imitation of Christ in his earthly poverty and self-humbling. This ideal seems to have been initiated—or at least its historic attraction for the Russian mind seems to have been initiated—by St. Theodosius (d. 1074), 'the first monastic saint canonized by the Russian church'; he has been called 'the first representative of Russian Kenoticism' (G. P. Fedotov, *A Treasury of Russian Spirituality* [London: Sheed & Ward, 1950]). Fedotov goes on: 'The ideal of the literal imitation of Christ in his poverty and humiliation on earth is an apprehension of religious genius which was to mould permanently the mentality of the Russian people . . . Far exceeding the limits of the kenotic ideal of St. Theodosius, it imprinted itself upon the mentality of the Russian people.' See also *The Humiliated Christ in Modern Russian Thought*, by N. Gorodetzky (London: S.P.C.K., 1938). So deeply rooted was this ideal, so independent of dogmatic presuppositions, that it continued to impose itself even upon Russian atheism. Its marked influence upon the great Russian literary men of the nineteenth century scarcely needs to be emphasized (Dostoievsky, Tolstoi, Gogol and others); and it remains one of the cardinal elements in virtually all Russian theological writing (Bulgakov, Soloviev, and many others).

See also G. P. Fedotov, *The Russian Religious Mind* (Cambridge, Mass.: Harvard Univ. Press, 1946), chapter iv, 'Russian Kenoticism'.

The form of a slave describes the fundamental condition of the life of man into which Christ entered, and defines the sense in which the 'self-emptying' is to be understood; the participle (aorist of 'coincident action'—Moulton, *op. cit.* 130 f.) is *epexegetic*. **Slave** is not to be taken as a reference to the humble estate of our Lord as the child of poverty, but to his acceptance of bondage under 'the Elemental Spirits of the universe', the *stoicheia* to whom all human life is subject, until it is set free by the redemptive act of Christ himself (Gal. iv. 3, 9; cf. Col. ii. 8, 20). As he was 'born under the law, to redeem those who were under the law' (Gal. iv. 4), so the thought here is that he was born into slavery to the Elemental Spirits, that

he might redeem those who were subject to the same thraldom
(see also the remarks of C. A. A. Scott, *op. cit.* p. 271). The
clause which follows—**being made in the likeness of men**—
simply generalizes and broadens the scope of the thought of his
participation in the life of humanity. **Likeness** (as in Rom.
viii. 3—see the note of C. K. Barrett, *ad loc.*) does not suggest
any degree of unreality in Christ's humanity; the word is almost
a synonym for 'form' (*morphē*) and 'image' (*eikōn*); but it
leaves room for the thought that the human likeness is not the
whole story. The second stanza of the strophe thus recites the
fact of the Incarnation: He who in pre-existence lived in a
condition of divine glory, condescended to assume the enslaved
condition of our humanity. There is no attempt to explain how
this transition could take place, or to explore the mystery of the
relation between **the form of God** and **the form of a slave.**
These are theological problems of the highest importance to us,
but the solution is not given to us within the words of our hymn.
The one thing indicated is that this Descent was *voluntary*; it is
not that God (or any other power) stripped him of his dignities
and prerogatives—he **stripped himself,** just as in the next
stanza we shall be told that he **humbled himself.** For the
same theological emphasis, cf. John x. 17-18.

Being made in the likeness of men should perhaps be
taken in the sense, 'being born into this world as all men are
born', as in Galatians iv. 4: 'God sent forth his Son, born of a
woman,' etc. Thus Joüon remarks with a good deal of force
that 'it would be strange if, in this evocation of the humiliation
of the Christ being made man, there was no intimation bearing
upon the mode of the Incarnation; seeing that elsewhere St.
Paul has underlined the similarity of the human origin of Christ
with that of other men' (he refers to Gal. iv. 4 and also to Rom.
i. 3). He suggests therefore that the participle γενόμενος should
be given its etymological (and not infrequent) sense of 'born',
and would render: 'né à l'instar des hommes' (*Notes philologiques*, p. 300). We would then have the thought of the *Te
Deum*: 'When thou tookest upon thee to deliver man, thou didst
not abhor the Virgin's womb'; though Paul, of course, makes no
mention of the virginity of the Mother of our Lord.

The third stanza of the strophe tells of his culminating act 8 in the human condition. **Found in shape as a man**—that is, with all the outward appearance of a man. Without any suggestion of discrepancy between the appearance and the underlying reality, room is left for the thought of something more within the human frame. **He humbled himself in becoming obedient unto death**—it must be noted again that both the main verb and the participle are aorists, and the participle is again epexegetic, setting forth more precisely what is meant by the self-humbling. The words do not describe a disposition, but an act of obedience. The contrast with Adam, as in Rom. v. 12-21, lies beneath the surface. L. Bouyer calls attention to the fact that 'in all the texts which are certainly and directly Pauline, wherein *anthrōpos* is applied to Christ, we observe that St. Paul compares him formally to Adam'; he mentions particularly Rom. v. 12-17 and 1 Cor. xv. 20-49 ('ΑΡΠΑΓΜΟΣ', in *RSR*, 39 [*Mélanges Jules Lebreton*], 1951-1952, pp. 281-288). Rom. v. 19 is especially pertinent: 'for as through the disobedience of the one man many were made sinners, so also through the obedience of the one many shall be made righteous'.

Obedient—it is not explicitly stated *to whom* the obedience is rendered. It is not certain that it means, as we would at first assume, to God. In the last analysis, of course, the will of God is fulfilled in the death of Christ ('this commandment have I received of my Father'—John x. 18); but it seems probable that the thought here bears rather upon his submission to the power of the Elemental Spirits. It is the part of the **slave** to be **obedient** to the one to whom he is committed (Rom. vi. 16 f.). A somewhat similar thought is expressed in Heb. ii. 14-15: Christ partook of the same flesh and blood as 'the children' whom God has given him, 'that through death he might destroy him who has the power of death, that is, the devil; and might deliver those who through fear of death were through all their lifetime subject to slavery'.

Death here signifies not alone the totality of Christ's obedience, but even more, in correspondence with the homage of the spirits of the underworld of which we shall hear in the second strophe, it carries with it the thought that the Redeemer in his Descent occupies the third realm of the universe, the realm of

death, the underworld. Within the frame of this thinking, the mode of his dying is not significant, but only the fact of **death** itself, which makes him one with the dead as he has made himself one with the living. 'For to this end Christ died and lived, that he might rule as lord over dead and living' (Rom. xiv. 9). **The death of the cross** belongs in Paul's own thinking to the economy of salvation, as the means of expiation, of redemption from the 'curse of the Law' (Gal. iii. 13); but the phrase here intrudes an element from a range of doctrine with which the hymn in itself is not concerned. Its presence as a Pauline gloss, which stands outside the formal structure of the hymn and is substantially irrelevant to its theme, is the chief indication that the hymn is not of Paul's own composition.

Second Strophe. In the first strophe, **Christ Jesus** is the acting subject all the way through; in the second strophe, it is God who acts and Christ is the object of the divine action. Two major antitheses govern the transition: (1) Humiliation —Exaltation; and (2) Slave—Lord. God has exalted him who humbled himself; God has given the Name of Lord (*Kyrios*— **the Name above every Name**) to him who took the form of a slave. The spirit-powers of the heavens, of the earth, and of the underworld now acclaim as Lord him who submitted to their tyranny as a slave.

Exalted him to the highest station—the unusual compound 9 verb (which we may render literally 'hyper-exalted') is given a superlative, not a comparative sense; the thought is not that God exalts him to a higher rank than he held before, as **being in the form of God.** No such comparison between the pre-existent state of Christ and his exalted state is envisaged. We must altogether reject the notion, widespread as it is among the commentators, that Christ received as the reward of his humility the high station of equality with God which he refused to seize for himself as plunder, by storming the heights like a Titan. The contrast is not between the pre-existent condition and the present exaltation; but between the earthly condition of slavery (self-humbling, obedience) and the consequent exaltation. Here is given, as it were, the archetypal pattern of the divinely-established law: 'whoever shall humble himself will be exalted' (Matt. xxiii. 11). It is *in his manhood* that Christ is now exalted and endued with all authority. Even the verb **conferred** ('granted as an act of grace') suggests that God is here dealing with Christ as *man*; cf. 1 Peter v. 5-6: 'God . . . gives grace to the humble'.

The Name—in ancient thought, not merely a designation to distinguish one individual from another, but an index of character and status. To grant **the Name that is above every name** is not merely to confer a high title of honour, but to commit plenary authority; it is parallel to the thought of Matthew xxviii. 18: 'All authority has been given to me in heaven and upon earth'.

10-11   The hymn now weaves into its structure some phrases from Isaiah xlv. 23: 'I have sworn by myself, the word is gone out of my mouth in righteousness and shall not return, That unto me every knee shall bow, every tongue shall swear'. This is part of an oracle that foretells the coming of God's everlasting salvation to all the world, and follows immediately upon the great appeal: 'Look unto me, and be ye saved, all the ends of the earth: for I am God, and there is none else'. The hymn affirms that this promise of world-wide acknowledgment of the saving sovereignty of God has been fulfilled in the exaltation of Christ. Its scope is extended still more widely; not only 'all the ends of the earth', but **dwellers in heaven and on earth and in the underworld** acclaim Jesus Christ as Lord. As always in the New Testament, the salvation of God embraces the entire cosmos, and homage is offered to the newly-crowned King by the mighty spirits who rule over its three realms. For it is not *human* adoration which the hymn describes, as if the threefold phrase meant 'the blessed dead in heaven, the living on earth, and the souls in purgatory'; all this would be the language of a later age. The reference here is certainly to *spirits*—astral, terrestrial, and chthonic. And the verb which we have rendered **acclaim** (AV, RSV, 'confess') has no reference to a confession of faith in Jesus on the part of *the church*. What is depicted here is an Enthronement—the Enthronement of Jesus Christ as the King of all God's creation, visible and invisible; and the acclamation of the spirits who surround his throne.

In the Name of Jesus—not *at* the Name, as if the utterance of the Name were the signal for the genuflection. As elsewhere, the phrase speaks of Jesus as the Mediator through whom created beings offer their worship to God. It is to *God* that every knee shall bow (cf. Eph. iii. 14: 'I bow my knees to the Father').

In this Exaltation of Jesus and the universal acclamation of his Lordship, there is no thought of any diminution of the honour of God, or any rivalry between divinities—a notion familiar enough in the surrounding paganism. It is God Himself who exalts Christ, and the acclamations which acknowledge his Enthronement redound **to the glory of God the Father.** The enthronement of Jesus and the conferring of the title of Lord mark his installation as God's vicegerent in the government of the universe. This is entirely in keeping with the Old Testament patterns of Messianic kingship. God Himself is the 'Shepherd' of Israel (a widely-used figure of kingship); yet this is quite compatible with the concomitant idea that God will make 'David' or a 'son of David' still to come, the Shepherd of his flock. Thus, for instance, in Ezekiel xxiv, God speaks of his own saving and protective care of his flock (vv. 11-16); but this quickly passes into the promise: 'I will set up one shepherd over them, and he shall feed them, even my servant David; he shall feed them, and he shall be their shepherd' (v. 23). So Mowinckel sets forth the general position: 'There is for the thought of Israel and the Old Testament no conflict between the kingly rule of Yahweh and that of the Messiah, just as, ideally, there is no conflict between Yahweh's kingly rule and that of His son, the anointed earthly king. . . . Naturally, thought may dwell on the one or the other of these two aspects, Yahweh's kingly rule, or his kingship as exercised through the future king; but they are never felt to be two distinct things' (S. Mowinckel, *He That Cometh*, tr. G. W. Anderson [Oxford: Blackwell, 1956], chap. vi, 'The Place of the King in the Future Hope: The Messiah', pp. 171-172). Theologically, the Fourth Gospel develops the theme that it is the will of the Father that all should honour the Son (John v. 19 f.). Lohmeyer draws attention to the universal Adoration of the Lamb (Apoc. v. 1-14), where the homage of 'everything created, in heaven and on earth and under the earth and in the sea, and all things that are in them' is offered in unison to 'the

Lamb that was slain', while all ascribe: 'Blessing and honour and glory and power to Him that is seated upon the throne and to the Lamb, for ever and ever'.

9. THIRD EXHORTATION: THE APOSTLE'S FAREWELL APPEAL. ii. 12-18

(12) So, my beloved, with fear and trembling work out your own salvation—just as you have always obeyed; not as in my presence only, but now much more in my absence; (13) for it is God who acts effectively among you, enabling you both to will and to act effectively for the accomplishment of his gracious will. (14) Do all without murmurings and arguments, (15) that you may become irreproachable and pure, blameless children of God in the midst of 'a crooked and perverse society'. Shine brightly among them, like stars in the world, (16) proferring the word of life, that you may be my pride against the Day of Christ that I have not run my course in vain or laboured in vain. (17) Indeed, even if my life is poured forth as a libation at the sacrifice and priestly service of your faith, I rejoice and share in joy with you all. (18) You too must likewise rejoice and share in joy with me.

All through this passage, Paul has in mind the farewell charge of Moses to the people whom he has led out of bondage and through the terrible wilderness with its perpetual menace to the very borders of the Promised Land (Deut. xxxii, esp. vv. 1-5; with the preparation in xxxi. 25-30). The very words of Deuteronomy xxxii. 5 are cited in v. 15 (from the Lxx text), with significant changes. The charge of Moses is clouded with reproach and the recollection of past disobedience: 'I know your contentiousness (*erethismos*, closely resembling the *eritheia*, 'partisanship', of i. 17 and ii. 3 above) and your stiff-necked stubbornness; for while I have still been with you in living presence, you have been constantly giving provocation

in the things pertaining to God; how shall you not do likewise
after my death?' (Deut. xxxi. 27, Lxx). The charge of Paul
begins with the thankful acknowledgment: 'You have always
obeyed'. Moses makes the bitter indictment:

'They have sinned, they are not his children,
    they are to be blamed,
They are a crooked and perverse society'
(Deut. xxxii. 5).

Paul uses the words but transforms the sentiment entirely,
when he urges his beloved Philippians to show themselves
children of God, blameless; and transfers the phrase **a
crooked and perverse society** to the surrounding paganism.
Even the **rejoice** of v. 18, identical in Greek with the word of
'Farewell!', intensifies the impression that this is indeed the
Apostle's farewell charge to the Philippians, and that he is
consciously thinking of the analogy between himself in his
prison, facing the prospect of death, and Moses in Moab;
knowing that he is leaving his people without his guidance and
counsel and that they must win through to the goal of their
long journey without any further help from him. But he is
confident of the issue, for God is still with them to fortify their
wills and to make their action effective **for the accomplishment of his gracious will.**

Just as you have always obeyed—as in v. 8 above, the 12
verb is used without an object. Here the sense is probably of
obedience to the gospel (2 Thess. i. 8), the obedience of faith
which the apostolic commission promotes (Rom. i. 5), or more
concretely of obedience to the Apostle's counsels and directions,
accepted as carrying all the authority of the God who gave him
the grace of the apostolate.

Not as in my presence only—the negative used here is
one which is not used with the indicative in the Greek of this
period; it must therefore be taken with the following verb
work out, not with **obeyed.** In the setting, the contrast of
presence and **absence** will be taken in the sense of 'during
my life', and 'after my death'. Like Moses, Paul speaks to
his people in the shadow of his impending departure from
this life; but where Moses looks back on a long record of

provocation, Paul looks back on an unbroken record of obedience.

Work out your own salvation. In such a context, where Paul thinks of himself as in the position of Moses, he thinks of the Philippians as in the position of Israel—delivered from the bondage of Egypt, safely conducted through the wilderness under his leadership, but with the final decisive stage still to be passed—the crossing of Jordan and the entrance into the Promised Land. This is the frame of thinking within which he throws out the challenge: **Work out your own salvation.** The **salvation** of which he speaks is here, as always, the eschatological fulfilment of the hope of the gospel, the winning through to the goal, the attainment of final blessedness. **Work out**—the verb has this sense of carrying the struggle on to its conclusion; enduring to the end, and so being saved. This **salvation** is still the gift of God, not the reward given to merit, even the merit of perseverance. But the part of the believer is not merely passive; he is called to exert himself actively to 'lay hold on eternal life' (1 Tim. vi. 12). The central emphasis in the clause falls certainly on the words **with fear and trembling** (K. Barth). In some sense, all Christian believers may be said to be working out their own salvation; the point of the injunction is that they should do so **with fear and trembling;** that is, with none of the complacency and spiritual self-satisfaction that thinks it can safely indulge in **partisanship** and **vain ambition,** and insistence on its own **rights** (vv. 3 and 4, above). Such **fear and trembling** is not caused by apprehension that God may turn against them at the last, that their hope of **salvation** is really precarious and insecure. It is prompted rather by the sense that it is *God* with whom they have to do, that they are constantly in his presence, that he is acting effectively among them and within them. So Paul, when he preached the Gospel at Corinth, was with them 'in weakness and in fear and in much trembling', not because he felt nervous before an audience or embarrassed by a lack of oratorical skill, but because he was profoundly conscious of the divine Spirit within him and around him, which gave his preaching its power to awaken faith (1 Cor. ii. 3 f.). Or again, the phrase may bear rather upon the spirit in which the Philippians should respond to admonitions, carrying as they do a measure of rebuke, addressed to them with the divine authority committed to the Apostle; compare the account of Titus' report of his work in the rebellious Corinthian church: 'recalling the obedience of you all, how you received him with fear and trembling' (2 Cor. vii. 15).

The phrase is used frequently in the Old Testament, almost always of the terror which the Israelites cause in their enemies (Deut. ii. 25; etc.).

Clearly enough, the recollection that it is **God who acts** 13 **effectively** among them could only fill them with assurance about the attainment of **salvation;** it could not conceivably be brought forward as a reason for fear and trembling lest they might fail.[1] This confirms the interpretation of **fear and trembling** as the awe inspired by a true sense of the divine presence. In part, the words are a solemn reminder that in Paul's absence as in his presence, God sustains and strengthens them; just as Moses charges Israel: 'Be courageous, be strong . . . for it is the Lord your God who goes forward with you and among you' (Deut. xxxi. 6, Lxx). The verb ἐνεργεῖ **(acts effectively)** has the same root as our word 'energy'; it is nearly always used of divine or supernatural action, and in the sense of causing action in someone else. The same verb is used of the effectual action which God inspires in his people—**(to will and) to act effectively**—as it were with a dynamic action that inspires action in others as well. **Among you**—the phrase can also mean simply 'in you'; but it seems better here to take it in the corporate sense, of the work of God in the life of the believing community. Paul is not speaking here of individual salvation; as throughout the epistle, he is concerned with the Philippian church in its corporate life and its corporate activity. This leads a number of commentators to take the last phrase of the verse in the sense 'to promote good will'—that is, friendliness and unity among the members of the community. But the noun *eudokia* and the cognate verb are nearly always used in the New Testament of the 'good will' of God—his royal 'pleasure'. (Joüon holds that it is 'quite clear grammatically that εὐδοκία refers to the subject of the clause, that is, to θεός').

[1] Cf. the paraphrase of Erasmus: 'Non est dormitationi aut securitati locus, sed rursum non est quod diffidatis'.

14 **Without murmurings and arguments.** Paul is still thinking of the failings of the Israelites in their journeyings through
the wilderness; in the same spirit, he warns the Corinthians
against falling into the faults of the ancient people of God and
incurring their punishment (1 Cor. x. 10: 'Do not murmur, as
some of them murmured, and were destroyed by the Destroyer'
—the reference is to Numbers xiv). **Arguments**—the word
thus rendered often means 'calculations, the casting of accounts';
this is a possible sense here also, making this a warning against
basing action upon calculations of worldly advantages to be
gained. Both words describe aspects of the self-assertive temper.

15 **Become**—perhaps simply 'show yourselves to be', 'be
manifestly'; but the stronger sense, conveying the thought of
character changed by divine grace, is probably justified in the
context of the epistle as a whole. The adaptation of phrases from
the Song of Moses in the following words has been noted above.

Shine brightly—the imperative appears to be required here,
rather than the indicative ('among whom you shine').

The words seem to carry a reminiscence of Daniel xii. 3
(Lxx): 'the wise shall shine as stars of the heaven'. There may
be also an influence of the dominical saying: 'Let your light so
shine before men, that they may see your good works and
glorify your Father who is in heaven' (Matt. v. 16).

In the world—the cosmos, not 'your neighbourhood, your
city', or even 'on earth'. There is a suggestion here of the
cosmic significance of the church of Christ (cf. Eph. iii. 10:
'that the manifold wisdom of God might now be made known
to the principalities and powers in the heavenly places through
the church'). But **the world** in New Testament usage of the
term means more often the world of human society, ordered in
hostility to God, though still the object of his love. Christian
believers are **stars,** set by God in their appointed place, as
tokens that he has not forsaken his alienated world. They are
points of heavenly light in the midst of the circumambient
darkness. Paul had travelled often enough by sea to know how
the sailor takes his reckoning by the stars and plots his course
to harbour through the darkness over the trackless waters.

16 **Proferring the word of life**—the participle shares the
imperative force of the governing verb. The light by which they

shine is **the word of life.** We have here a striking parallelism
of expression to the Prologue of the Fourth Gospel; where
again *logos* ('word'), *kosmos* ('world'), and *zōē* ('life') are
brought together in relation to the revelation of God in Christ.
'In (the Logos) was life, and the life was the light of men; and
the light shines in the darkness and the darkness has not
extinguished it' (John i. 4-5). **The word of life** in our passage,
however, cannot be taken in the personal sense, as of Christ
himself (though this thought is not too far removed). It will
mean rather 'the Gospel', as the word of God which brings
light and life to all who receive it 'not as a word of men, but as
it truly is, the word of God, which acts effectively in (those)
who believe' (1 Thess. ii. 13). It is clear that the words cannot
mean the holy scriptures as such; in an age of manuscripts, the
Philippians were not in a position to pass out copies of the
Septuagint as a means of evangelization! It must be kept in
mind that the New Testament books were not yet written,
except for a few epistles of Paul; and these were not regarded
as holy scripture either by him or by his churches. The Bible
of the early church consisted wholly of the Old Testament
scriptures in Greek; the Jews had these also, and the Hebrew
texts as well, but that did not lead Paul to think of them as
stars in the world.

Paul has always before him the vision of **the Day of Christ,** 16
when he will be called to give the final reckoning of the task
entrusted to him. He has the strongest sense of responsibility
as a 'steward of the mysteries of God' (1 Cor. iv. 1 ff.). If the
Philippians heed his appeal, he will be able to point to them as
evidence of his faithful discharge of his stewardship: they will
be his **pride,** the demonstration that his work has not been
done **in vain.**

The Apostle now makes use of a series of terms drawn from 17
the vocabulary of priesthood and sacrifice. The **libation** was a
drink-offering, usually a cup of wine, poured out on the ground
to honour Deity; such offerings were frequent in both Jewish
and pagan worship. Paul is again referring to the prospect of
martyrdom which he faces, and thinks of himself, his life's
blood, as a **libation** poured forth to God. If he must die at the
hands of the public executioner, he offers his life to God as a

tribute of love and gratitude. **At the sacrifice**—perhaps 'to crown the sacrifice', perhaps 'to initiate it' (the rites of libation frequently preceded other sacrifices). **Sacrifice and priestly service** is probably to be taken as hendiadys—the offering of the sacrifice is the proper function of the priest. **Your faith** can hardly be understood as expressing the matter of the sacrifice which is to be offered, but rather as the source of the impulse to make the offering. **Faith** in God finds its true expression in the **priestly service** of offering **sacrifice** to him. The sacrifice which the Christian offers is first of all himself (Rom. xii. 1— 'I beseech you . . . to present your bodies as a living sacrifice . . . which is your spiritual service'); then his substance (2 Cor. ix. 12), his prayers, and his activities. The entire life of the Christian church is represented in the New Testament generally as 'a holy work of priesthood', appointed 'to offer spiritual sacrifices acceptable to God through Jesus Christ' (1 Pet. ii. 5). There may be here a specific reference to the supplies which the Philippians have sent to Paul through Epaphroditus—in the sense that these constitute the sacrifice which their faith has prompted them to make (cf. ii. 30, below).

The prospect of death, so envisaged, is not a cause for grief, but for joy. Paul feels no dismay himself, and he will not have his friends dismayed. They are making their sacrifice with joy, and he rejoices with them; if his life is to be a libation, he will 18 rejoice in his sacrifice, and he calls them to **rejoice and share in joy** with him.

(d) ANNOUNCEMENT OF PLANS. ii. 19-30

10. THE APOSTLE HOPES TO SEND TIMOTHY, AND TO COME LATER HIMSELF : EPAPHRODITUS IS RETURNING AT ONCE, AND THE APOSTLE COMMENDS HIM HIGHLY. ii. 19-30

(19) I hope, in the Lord Jesus, to send Timothy to you shortly, so that I too may be cheered by getting knowledge of your state. (20) For I have no one of qualities

like his, who will be sincerely concerned for your state.
(21) They are all looking after their own affairs, not the
things of Christ Jesus. (22) But his proven worth you know,
how as a son with a father he has served with me in the
propagation of the gospel. (23) Him, then, I hope to send
at once, as soon as I see the outcome of my present
situation; (24) and I am confident, in the Lord, that I shall
come soon myself also. (25) But I think it necessary to
send to you Epaphroditus, my brother and fellow worker
and companion in arms, whom you sent with your
commission to execute your service to me in my need;
(26) for he has been longing for you all, and has been
troubled because you heard that he fell sick. (27) And in
fact he did fall sick; he was near death; but God took pity
on him, and not only on him but on me also, lest I should
have sorrow upon sorrow. (28) The more eagerly, therefore, do I send him, so that you may see him and be glad
again, and that I may be less sorrowful. (29) Welcome
him in the Lord, therefore, with all joy; and hold men
like him in honour. (30) For he came near death for the
sake of the work of Christ, risking his life to fulfil what you
could not fulfil in this service for me.

It is obvious that when Paul wrote these words he had not
the slightest intention of adding further long paragraphs of
warning and exhortation. He is bringing his letter to an end.
It remains to be asked whether the two chapters which follow
are to be regarded as a postscript or series of postscripts, added
before the letter was despatched; or whether it is in whole or
in part a fragment from another letter, which became attached
to this letter when the correspondence of Paul was collected
and edited for publication. These questions are discussed in the
Introduction, under 'Authenticity and Integrity of the Epistle'.

Paul is sending Epaphroditus along with the letter, without
waiting until his own case is disposed of. He knows that the
Philippians will be anxious to know the outcome of his trial,
and so he promises that as soon as it is known, he will send
Timothy with the news; and if he is set free, as he thinks he
may, he will come himself soon afterwards. But he has decided

to send Epaphroditus on his way without waiting for the final disposition of his case, because he has been sick, he knows that the Philippians have heard about his sickness, and he is eager to see them and to let them see him, to dispel any lingering anxiety over his health that may be in their minds. Timothy will come soon afterwards, not only to bring the news about Paul but also to help them as only one deeply concerned could help, and to bring back word which the Apostle hopes will be cheering to him—word of dissensions overcome, of partisan-ship and vain ambition laid aside, of a church united against the common foe and at one with itself and with Christ. The thought offers no difficulty, and only a few details require comment.

19   **In the Lord Jesus.** The Apostle's hopes and plans are not formed idly, or at the prompting of his own desires or wisdom, but in the full consciousness of his union in life with Christ. **The Lord Jesus** is the sphere, the medium in which he thinks and acts.

20   **I have no one of qualities like his.** The **qualities** which the Apostle has in mind are not Timothy's general gifts, but the capacity to be concerned for the well-being of others. It is possible that the sentence should be rendered, 'I have no one else who so shares my mind', the adjective 'equal-souled' (ἰσόψυχον) being taken in the sense 'equal to me in soul' 'equally concerned with me for your welfare', rather than 'equal to him in soul', as in our translation **of qualities like his.** Both senses are good: 'I have no one to match him', or 'I have no one else who can fill my shoes, for the task in hand'. Joüon (*Notes philologiques*, p. 302) argues strongly for the sense 'no one who shares my sentiments', on the ground that the Apostle is using the language of Psalm liv (lv). 13: 'Thou, a man mine equal' (ἰσόψυχε). This is the only occurrence of the word in the Greek Old Testament, but if Paul had this passage in mind, he must have forgotten the context, for this 'man of equal soul' is reproached for betraying his friend. Note the paraphrase of Erasmus: 'Hunc igitur velut alterum me mittam'.

    Your state—literally, 'the things concerning you'. Probably Paul is not satisfied that he has a clear and true picture of the spiritual condition of the Philippian church. He is, of course, dependent upon reports from visitors, which may be coloured by their own personal sympathies. He hopes that the seriousness of the dissensions has been exaggerated in the representations made to him; he fears that things may be worse than he imagines. Timothy will be able to inform him more soberly; and his 'concern' for them will lead him to take measures to restore harmony. Paul is not sending him as a fact-finding commission merely, but as a responsible and trusted lieutenant, who will press home the appeals made in the letter.

All—naturally, not all the Christians of the local church; for 21 many of them are preaching the gospel boldly, with love (i. 16). He is not charging the entire community with selfish unconcern for **the things of Christ Jesus** (in the instance, this must mean, for the work that is to be done for Christ in restoring harmony at Philippi). He is speaking of such men as he might have charged with the mission on which he is now sending Timothy. Perhaps he had already asked some of them to go to Philippi, and had met with one refusal after another, given on grounds that seemed to him unworthy of Christian leaders. He undoubtedly expected a great deal of people; they may well have felt that he expected too much, when he asked them to drop **their own affairs** for weeks, perhaps for months on end, while they made the long journey to Philippi.

His proven worth you know. They will not feel that they 22 are being sent any mediocre substitute. Timothy was with Paul when he first brought the gospel to Philippi (Acts xvi).

Confident . . . that I shall soon come myself. Again we 24 see how his mind fluctuates between the expectation of death and the prospect of being set again at liberty; almost from moment to moment his outlook seems to change. But there is never the slightest hint of worry, let alone panic. The peace of Christ reigns in his heart.

I think—the English present renders the Greek epistolary 25 aorist; the writer projects himself as it were into the time when the letter will be read.

Epaphroditus is not known to us except through this epistle. He is not to be identified with the Epaphras of Colossae. The name is of pagan origin, being formed on the name of the Greek goddess Aphrodite. Epaphroditus must have come of a Greek

family devoted to her cult. Christians of later times did not
hesitate to retain these names of pagan origin in their families—
there are plenty of Christian Isidores and Sarapions.

Companion in arms (fellow soldier) is of course meta-
phorical; they are both soldiers of Christ.

Whom you sent with your commission—literally, 'your
apostle'. The term is not confined to a limited group of missionaries, though it is used in a special sense of the Twelve and a
somewhat wider circle who were charged with certain unique
functions at the beginning of the church. This special sense is
not found here. However, it should be said that apostle is not a
regular Greek word for 'commissioner', or 'representative'; in
profane Greek, it is rarely used of persons at all. The New
Testament usage is substantially a new departure, coined to
render a Jewish term. (See *BKW*, 'Apostleship'.) Epaphroditus
is commissioned by the church, and his task is conceived as
priestly: he is their 'apostle and *leitourgos*' (its cognate *leitourgia*
—our 'liturgy'—is found in ii. 17 and 30)—'minister', with
definite connotations of 'one who does priestly service'. It is
not suggested that Epaphroditus was a 'priest' in the technical
sense of one admitted to an order of priesthood; but that the
generous gift which he brought from Philippi was a sacrificial
offering (cf. iv. 18, with its wealth of sacrificial terminology), and
the bringer does a priestly **service** on their behalf.

26   **You heard that he fell sick.** Evidently there has been time,
since the arrival of Epaphroditus, for word of his illness to get
to Philippi and also for a return message. This is one of the
main points in the argument brought against the likelihood
that the letter was written from Rome, which was more than
eight hundred miles from Philippi; the journey would require
several weeks, each way. The argument is not conclusive; it is
clear that if Epaphroditus could have slipped back for a week-
end, there would not be all this circumstantial discussion about
his return. A fairly long journey is presupposed. The journey
from Ephesus, of course, would take several days; Paul and his
party spent at least ten days at sea on the way from Philippi to
Miletus (Acts xx. 6, 13-15).

27   **Sorrow upon sorrow**—probably simply sorrow at the death
of Epaphroditus, added to sorrow at his critical illness.

The more eagerly—perhaps, 'the more hastily', even 28 'somewhat prematurely'. The Apostle may be concerned to ward off criticism of Epaphroditus for leaving him before his release from prison. It is he who has made the decision to send him back, that the Philippians may be relieved of all anxiety over the state of his health. But how should St. Paul be thereby **less sorrowful?** Perhaps in the sense that he will be less anxious about the state of the Philippian church once he knows that his trusted **fellow worker and companion in arms** is there to rally them and resolve their petty dissensions.

Hold men like him in honour. For he came near death 29, 30 **for the sake of the work of Christ.** Epaphroditus has earned new titles to their respect and confidence, which should strengthen his hand in dealing with their difficulties.

The work of Christ—the specific task for which the Philip- 30 pians sent him is here viewed as the work which Christ has given him to do.

Risking his life—a striking phrase, actually taken from the language of the gambler; almost, 'he gambled with his life as the stake'. The words are too strong to be taken as a mere reference to the sickness of Epaphroditus; they suggest some hazard to which he exposed himself, which might well have cost him his life.

To fulfil what you could not fulfil. This is a paraphrase; the literal rendering would be 'to fulfil the deficiency'. But such a literal rendering would misrepresent the thought. The words do not convey any shadow of rebuke; there is no suggestion that the Philippians have fallen short of their Christian duty to Paul. The same word for 'deficiency' is used (in the plural) in Colossians i. 24 (a well-known *crux interpretum*): 'I fulfil the deficiencies of Christ's afflictions', where there is certainly no suggestion that Christ has not suffered enough afflictions in his own person! The Philippians could send gifts to Paul in his prison; the only 'deficiency' is that they could not be with him themselves, to do him service. This is the 'deficiency' that Epaphroditus has fulfilled by his personal attentions.

Service—once again, the offering of the church and the work of its commissioner are conceived as '*priestly*'.

CHAPTER THREE

(e) CONCLUSION AND POSTSCRIPT (commenced). iii. 1

**(1a) Finally, my brethren, I bid you farewell in the Lord.
(1b) [To repeat the same pleas to you need not cause me
trepidation, and for you it is safe.]**

Paul has finished his letter and begins to say his farewells;
but interrupts himself to add a direct appeal to two women of
the Philippian church. See section 13, below.

If any justification of the rendering **farewell** is required (in
place of 'rejoice', which is given in AV and RSV, but is certainly
wrong in this context), see the discussion of Professor E. J.
Goodspeed in his *Problems of New Testament Translation*,
pp. 174 f.; cf. the note on iv. 4, below.

II.—AN INTERPOLATED FRAGMENT. iii. 2-21

I T is evident that at this point we come to an abrupt break in
the course of the letter. Many scholars are prepared to accept
this as a mark of the unstudied character of a personal letter;
the writer is not composing an essay, and feels free to go off at
a tangent, as new thoughts arise in his mind. It is suggested by
some that Paul may have been interrupted and compelled to
suspend dictation for some time; and before he resumed, he may
have received word of Jewish proselytizing activities among the
Philippian Christians, which caused him to burst forth with
fierce invectives. But any such hypothesis seems to do less than
justice to the seriousness of the break and the complete lack of
connection between this chapter and the remainder of the letter.
This section appears to presuppose conditions and dangers of
which there is not so much as a hint in the other three chapters.

100

It can hardly be doubted that we have here a fragment of another letter, undoubtedly a letter of Paul's, but written on a different occasion and for a different purpose.

The fragment falls into two main divisions. In the first (iii. 2-16), the Apostle is dealing with a type of Jewish propaganda which seeks to win Gentile converts to Christianity over to Judaism, on the ground that 'perfection' is only to be attained through incorporation into the Jewish community. He refutes this by pointing to his own example; born into the Jewish inheritance in its fullness, and having made proof of the highest attainments within it, he had cast aside all its supposed advantages and everything else that men commonly count advantageous, for the sake of winning Christ. He does not make any claim that in Christ he has attained perfection, but he devotes himself unceasingly to progress towards this goal. In the second division (iii. 17-iv. 1), he warns against the shameful conduct of voluptuaries, whose whole outlook is limited to earthly things. He reminds his readers that the Christian homeland is in heaven, holds before them the hope of the coming of the Lord as the Saviour who will transform us into his glorious likeness, and bids them stand firm in the Lord.

There is no means of discovering where and when the letter containing this fragment was written. We cannot even be certain that it was written to the church of Philippi; there are indeed some considerations which might lead us to think of some other church as its destination. There were few Jews in Philippi; so few that they had no synagogue, but met for prayers in a place by the river outside the city gate (Acts xvi. 13); accordingly, it was not a city in which one would expect Jewish proselytizing activity to be a danger so pressing as to call forth the savage invective of verse 2. On the other hand, we may reasonably feel that if the fragment is found in a letter to the Philippians, it will be because the collector of the Pauline letters found it in the church chest at Philippi. Yet he seems to have attached to the epistle to the Romans a letter which was originally sent to the church of Ephesus (Rom. xvi. 1-23). He was certainly capable of weaving fragments from several letters into one, as is seen most clearly in 2 Corinthians, but in that case there is no reason to doubt that all the parts belong to his correspondence with the church of Corinth. We must regard it as probable that our fragment likewise belongs to his correspondence with the church of Philippi. In any case, it must be interpreted in and for itself, without relation to its immediate context and without any knowledge of the time and circumstances of its composition.

The place of verse 1b is uncertain. Some editors attach it to 1a (rendered by them, 'rejoice in the Lord'); others take it as a kind of introduction to the invective of verse 2. The present writer would suggest that it belongs more naturally after the interpolation, as an introduction to the appeal to Evodia and Syntyche (iv. 2). See the note, *ad loc.*

11. A WARNING AGAINST JEWISH PROPAGANDA; PAUL'S RENUNCIATION OF JUDAISM, AND DEVOTION TO CHRIST. iii. 2-16

(2) Beware of the dogs, beware of the malicious labourers, beware of the incision. (3) For it is we who are the circumcision, we who worship by the Spirit of God, and take pride only in Christ Jesus and have not put our confidence in flesh,—(4) even though I have grounds for putting confidence in flesh; if any other man supposes that he may put confidence in flesh, I have better grounds than he. (5) For I was circumcised on the eighth day, I was a child of the race of Israel, of the tribe of Benjamin, a Hebrew born of Hebrew parents; in the matter of the Law, a Pharisee; (6) in the matter of zeal, a persecutor of the church; in the matter of righteousness (the righteousness which rests on the Law), proven blameless. (7) But such things, which were once gain to me, I have counted as loss for the sake of Christ. (8) Not only that, but I count everything as loss for the sake of the supreme good, the knowledge of Christ Jesus my Lord, for whose sake I forfeited everything and count it all rubbish that I may gain Christ (9) and be found in him; not having a righteousness of my own (the kind of righteousness which

issues from Law) but the righteousness which is given through faith in Christ—the righteousness which proceeds from God and is accorded to faith; (10) to the end that I may come to know him and the power of his resurrection and fellowship of his sufferings; conforming myself to his death (11) if only I may attain to the resurrection from the dead. (12) Not that I have already won the prize or have already attained perfection; but I speed on in the hope that I may win, just as I have been won by Christ Jesus. (13) Brethren, I do not reckon that I have won; but I hold to the one object: forgetting the things that are behind me and straining eagerly towards the things that lie ahead, (14) I speed on towards the finish line, to win the prize of the high vocation to which God has called me in Christ Jesus.

(15) Let all of us who are perfect be so disposed; if you look on things at all differently, this too will God reveal to you. (16) Only, at the point which we have already reached, we must stand in line by that.

Paul seldom launches into such vicious invective as here; 2 only in the imprecations of his letter to the Galatians do we find the same heat of passion (Gal. i. 8-9; and especially v. 12). **The dogs** is undoubtedly an epithet hurled at the Jews (!), his own people, for whom he has nevertheless a deep and abiding love (Rom. x. 1: 'My heart's desire and prayer to God for them is for their salvation'; and Rom. ix. 3: 'I could pray that I myself might be accursed from Christ on behalf of my brethren, my kinsmen according to the flesh'). He turns against them the scornful term which they were accustomed to apply to the Gentiles. The phrase may have been suggested to him by the common Latin warning sign, *Cave canem* ('Beware of the dog'). But he is not thinking of watchdogs who guard their master's property, but of the half-savage dogs who prowl about a camp and steal any food that is left unguarded. Jewish missioners who prowl around the Christian congregations, seeking to win Gentile converts over to Judaism, are compared to these scavenger **dogs.** Such bitterness is not, of course, directed against all or nearly all Jews, but against the fanatics who would 'compass sea and land to make one proselyte, and when he is made . . . make him twofold more the child of hell' than themselves (Matt. xxiii. 15).

Malicious labourers—the noun is used frequently, almost technically, of the Christian missionaries, the 'labourers' whom God sends forth into his harvest (Matt. ix. 38). Used of the Jewish propagandists, the phrase suggests that they are carrying on a kind of parody of the Christian mission, working to bring harm to men in place of everlasting salvation. The adjective (*kakos*) is one of the broadest words for 'evil', 'bad', 'wicked' in Greek; but often has the particular sense of **malicious**—bent on doing evil to others. Paul shows clearly enough in his letter to the Galatians that the Christian endangers his whole relationship with Christ and with God when he allows himself to be seduced by the doctrine that he needs anything besides faith in Christ for his justification (Gal. v. 1-5). Those who would require him to be circumcised and to keep the Law of Moses, therefore, are working for his hurt and shame.

Incision—the Greek word used here (*katatomē*) is a parody on the similar word for circumcision (*peritomē*); the Latin versions attempted to reflect this wordplay by coining the word *concisio*, to match *circumcisio*; and our Authorized Version has simply transliterated the Latin as 'concision'. The word has no established meaning; perhaps 'mutilation' would best give the sense. It is a somewhat vulgar jeer, intended to suggest that the rite of circumcision, valued by the Jew as the outward sign of his membership in the holy community, is in fact nothing more than a mangling of his body. **The circumcision** was to the Jew a proud title, used in the sense of 'the people of the circumcision', the community that has been set apart for God's own possession. Paul denies this title to the Jews and replaces it with the jeering title, of his own coinage, **the incision,** or 'the people of the mutilation'.

3   The title which he denies to the Jews, he claims for the Christians. **It is we who are the circumcision.** The true significance of circumcision does not lie in the outward operation, but in the inward consecration of which it should be the emblem. The whole conception is spiritualized. The same underlying thought is more fully expressed in Romans ii. 28-29:

'For the true Jew is not he who is outwardly a Jew, nor is the true circumcision that which is an outward matter, done in the flesh; but the true Jew is he who is a Jew inwardly, and the true circumcision is circumcision of the heart, in spirit not in the letter'. This spiritualizing re-interpretation goes back at least to Jeremiah, in his challenge to his people: 'Circumcise yourselves to the Lord, and take away the foreskins of your hearts, ye men of Judah and inhabitants of Jerusalem' (Jer. iv. 4). Elsewhere Paul can speak of Baptism as the Christian circumcision 'made without hands' (Col. ii. 11 f.). Here there is no reference, direct or implied, to Baptism; but the Christian right to the title of **the circumcision** is grounded in the realities of Christian spiritual experience, in worship and in faith.

We who worship by the Spirit of God—the phrase is very difficult, and its awkwardness has led to the creation of simplifying variant readings ($\theta\epsilon o \hat{v}$—'of God' is altered to the dative $\theta\epsilon\hat{\omega}$, making it the object of the participle—'worship God in spirit'; in the Beatty papyrus, our earliest witness, the word for 'God' is omitted altogether). The sense is perhaps better taken as 'we who worship in spirit—the spirit which God has given us'. The contrast between a true spiritual worship and mere external ordinances certainly lies near the surface; there is a close parallelism with the Johannine contrast between the worship 'in spirit and in truth' which the Father seeks, and the temple-rites of Jerusalem and of Samaria alike, which have but a transitory significance (John iv. 21-24). The true 'people of the circumcision' are those who offer this spiritual worship by the Spirit of God. By implication, any truly spiritual character, hence any ultimate validity, is denied to Jewish ordinances.

Take pride only in Christ Jesus—not, that is to say, in any heritage of Law or privilege of race; in contrast with the man who 'gives himself the title of Jew and rests complacently upon the Law and takes pride in God and knows His will' (Rom. ii. 17 f.; cf. 1 Cor. i. 26-31). Saul the Pharisee took pride in his Jewish inheritance and in himself as a devout and accomplished scion of Judaism (Gal. i. 13-14); now he **takes pride** in no religious insight or moral achievement of his own, but **only in Christ Jesus.**

Confidence in flesh—there is a side reference to circumcision, as an external mark 'made in the flesh by hands' (Eph. ii. 11); but **flesh** has the broader sense of *human privilege and achievement*—everything, even the best and highest, of which man is capable in himself, or in association with others, without utter and absolute dependence upon God. It is this self-reliance, this confidence in his own capacity to please God and earn a favourable verdict from the Judge, which vitiates the religion of the Jew even when he follows it with the most devoted zeal for God and the most sincere striving to fulfil his Law. 'For they being ignorant of God's righteousness, and going about to establish their own righteousness, have not submitted themselves unto the righteousness of God' (Rom. x. 3). **Have not put our confidence in flesh** is the statement in negative terms of the positively expressed **take pride only in Christ Jesus.**

Paul will not allow any misunderstanding of his position. If he thinks little of personal advantages of birth and rearing, it is 4 not because he himself does not possess them. **If any other man supposes that he may put confidence in flesh, I have better grounds than he.** He will not have it thought that he is decrying cultural and religious distinctions of other people, to which he can make no claim. On the contrary, if there is to be a competition in such distinctions, it is he who will emerge at the head of the list. He proceeds to list his claims to distinction.

5 **Circumcised on the eighth day**—according to the provision of the law (Lev. xii. 3); indicating that he came of a family meticulous in its fulfilment of the prescribed duties, and also that he is no proselyte, circumcised after his conversion; he belongs to Israel from birth. Possibly some of the **malicious workers** whom he has in mind were proselytes, doubly zealous for their adopted faith, now ready to boast of their circumcision and to urge others to follow their example. **Of the race of Israel**—possessing by birth all the privileges of the chosen people. **Of the tribe of Benjamin**—this probably is reflected in his Hebrew name of Saul, after the first of the kings, who was a man of Benjamin. It is not necessary to suppose that this tribe was acknowledged to have any particular distinction; Paul is reciting his titles of honour, as he regarded them before he

became a Christian, and a man of Benjamin would naturally take pride in his own tribe. **A Hebrew born of Hebrew parents**—probably included as an additional mark of distinction, from the side of 'flesh'—he came of a family which had not succumbed to its environment by forgetting its ancestral language; a family which continued to speak Aramaic (often referred to as 'Hebrew'—e.g., Acts xxi. 40) even after long years of settlement in a Greek city; in some parts of Canada, Scottish families still pride themselves on preserving the Gaelic speech of their forebears who emigrated from the Western Highlands three or four generations ago. In answer to a form of Jewish propaganda which insists that the blessings of God are promised only to such as become members of the Jewish national community, Paul replies that he was born into all the privileges that Judaism could give and that he attaches no value to them whatever.

Born with all these advantages of racial and religious inheritance, he has improved them by the practice of earnest piety and fanatical zeal. **In the matter of the Law, a Pharisee**—that is, a member of the sect which was most strict in its adherence to the Law, oral and written: 'a body of Jews who profess to be more religious than the rest, and to explain the laws more precisely', as Josephus puts it. 'The Pharisees were a party whose endeavour it was to live in strict accordance with the law thus interpreted and amplified (by the study and exposition of the Scribes, and the Tradition of interpretation which they had established), and to bring the people to a similar conformity' (G. F. Moore, *Judaism in the First Centuries of the Christian Era*, vol. i [Cambridge, Mass.; Harvard University Press, 1927], p. 66). Paul does not use the name **Pharisee** as a reproach, but as a title of honour; and the Pharisees were in fact highly regarded by the masses of the people. If the word has become in our own usage an epithet of scorn, a synonym for the sanctimonious hypocrite, this is undoubtedly due to the impression made upon us by the stinging indictment of 'scribes and Pharisees' which is attributed to our Lord in the Gospels, especially in the Gospel according to St. Matthew. Who can forget those searing words: 'Woe unto you, scribes and Pharisees, hypocrites! for you shut up the kingdom of heaven against men

. . . you devour widow's houses and for a pretence make long
prayers; . . . you are like whitewashed tombs, which indeed
appear beautiful outwardly, but within are full of dead men's
bones. . . . So you outwardly appear righteous to men, but
inwardly you are full of hypocrisy and lawlessness' (Matt.
xxiii. 13, 14, 27)? But Paul does not think of himself and of the
Pharisees who had been his teachers and associates for many
years in any such terms as these. Certainly he himself was no
hypocrite, nor were the great rabbis, all of them Pharisees,
whose names and sayings have been transmitted to us. When he
tells us that he was **in the matter of the Law, a Pharisee,**
he is claiming the highest degree of faithfulness and sincerity in
the fulfilment of his duty to God as prescribed by the divinely-
given Torah.

6   **In the matter of zeal, a persecutor of the church.**
Ironical, as the words of a Christian; but utterly serious, according to the standards of judgment of the faithful Pharisee. Paul's
whole conception of the relation between Christianity and Judaism is determined by the fact that his ancestral religion, *faith-
fully practised*, led him into the incredible, appalling position
of a **persecutor of the church** of God! It was not because he
was a bad Jew, untrue to the best traditions of his faith, that
he became a persecutor; it was precisely because of his ardent
fidelity to his faith that he sought by every means in his power
to destroy the Christian movement. As soon as he became
convinced that the Christians whom he was persecuting,
imagining that he was doing God service, were in fact God's
people; and that the crucified One whom they worshipped as
Lord was in fact the promised Messiah, raised from the dead by
God; then he was bound to make a radical, penetrating criticism
of the religion which had led him into this enormity. It is not
surprising, then, that he reacted so violently against any suggestion that the Judaism, which he knew so well, and in which he
had shown himself so proficient, could possibly be needed to
supplement the Gospel, when it had actually made him into a
persecutor of the Gospel. Compare Galatians i. 13-14: 'You
have heard of my former life in Judaism, how I persecuted the
church of God beyond all measure, and ravaged it—and I was
making progress in Judaism beyond many of my own age in my

nation, being exceedingly zealous for my ancestral traditions'. It was simply inconceivable to him that anyone could propose in good faith that Gentile converts to Christianity should be schooled in the very Judaism which he had renounced.

In the matter of righteousness (the righteousness which rests on the Law), proven blameless. Blameless— according to standards of **righteousness** which attached no blame to the persecution of the church of God! He is far from thinking that in meeting the standards of such a righteousness, he was blameless in the sight of God. The expression is quite consistent with his teaching, given repeatedly elsewhere, that 'all have sinned and come short of the glory of God', and that 'by the works of the Law shall no flesh be justified in his sight' (Rom. iii. 23, 20). **The righteousness which rests on the Law** measures itself by inadequate and fundamentally erroneous standards (2 Cor. x. 12). These standards can be met, and Paul is claiming that as a devout Pharisee, he met them—and yet he was persecuting the church! We have here a particular application given to the warning of Jesus; 'I tell you, unless your righteousness exceeds the righteousness of the scribes and Pharisees, you will not enter into the kingdom of heaven' (Matt. v. 20). It is not a matter of a higher degree of the same kind of righteousness, as if we were called to outdo the Pharisees in zeal for the Law. It is a matter of a different kind of righteous-ness, as Paul will make clear in a moment—**the righteousness which proceeds from God and is accorded to faith.**

It has been assumed that the opponents whom Paul is here attacking are non-Christian Jews; but it is possible (as is held by many commentators) that they are Christians of the Juda-izing faction of the early Palestinian church, who appear to have carried on a kind of counter-apostolate against Paul among his Gentile churches in Syria, in Galatia and in Achaea, denying his right to call himself an Apostle, claiming superior rights and privileges for themselves, and boasting of their Hebrew prerogatives. They certainly preached that Gentile converts must be circumcised, if they were to be saved. Such were the people whose claims he challenges in 2 Corinthians xi. 16-33, in a passage which has remarkable similarities with the language of our fragment.

'Since many are boasting on grounds of flesh, I too will boast. . . . Are they Hebrews? So am I. Are they Israelites? So am I. Are they descendants of Abraham? So am I. Are they servants of Christ? I say it like a man out of his wits, but I am their superior in that—I can beat them in the weight of my toils, in the number of times I have been in jail, in the lashings I have suffered, often in the last extremity' (vv. 18, 22-23).

The Corinthians had allowed themselves to be gulled by the arrogant claims of these 'super-apostles', as Paul calls them (2 Cor. xi. 13)—though he gives his true judgment of them without irony when he declares that they are 'false apostles, guileful labourers, masquerading as apostles of Christ'; he will even say that they are ministers of Satan, who 'disguise themselves as ministers of righteousness' (2 Cor. xi. 13-14). There is no indication that they have had any success as yet among the readers to whom our fragment was addressed, whether Philippians or not; there is nothing here resembling the torrents of reproach and pleading which Paul pours out upon the Corinthian church. Instead, he turns at once, after this short burst of invective and irony, to a most moving confession of the springs and aspirations of his own inward life—a life for which his inherited standards of righteousness and grounds of pride were wholly irrelevant—actually, indeed, handicaps to the one kind of progress by which he now sets store.

7 **Such things, which were once gain to me, I have counted as loss for the sake of Christ.** We might almost adopt here the very words of Aristotle: 'These terms "loss" and "gain" are borrowed from the language of voluntary barter' (*Eth. Nic.* v. iv. 13, 1132 b). Paul is using the figure of a balance-sheet, showing Assets and Liabilities. All these advantages of birth and upbringing, he had formerly set down in the column of Assets; now he has transferred them to the column of Liabilities. Certainly this is an extreme way of putting it; but he means to make it clear that so long as a man keeps thinking of his own personal advantages, inherited or acquired, as giving him a better standing before God, all such things are disadvantages to him. Far from advancing him along the road to 'perfection', they hold him back. For it is the way of God to

create out of nothing, to choose 'the foolish things of the world that he may put the wise to shame . . . the weak things of the world that he may put the strong to shame . . . the base things of the world, things that count for nothing, yes, things that are not, that he may reduce to nothingness the things that are; to the end that no flesh may boast in the presence of God' (1 Cor. i. 27-29).

I count everything as loss—everything, that is, which he 8 would once have counted as an advantage to him; perhaps he thinks specifically of the privileges of Roman citizenship; perhaps more generally of an assured position in the world, of the respect of his teachers and comrades, of material possessions. Even the things which are most desirable in themselves become worthless in comparison with **the supreme good of the knowledge of Christ.** For the attainment of the highest end in life, he is wholly dependent upon God; he has no accumulated spiritual capital in his own possession. Anything and everything which he can call his own, and regard with pride, he counts **as loss.**

In a more general context, Karl Barth has written: 'We are to understand, therefore, that for God to be revealed involves the dislodging of man from the estimation of his own freedom, and his enrichment with the freedom of the children of God. This negation, the negation of man through God's eternal grace and mercy, is only the obverse of his position as a child of God, as a member of the covenant between God and man. Thus God's possibility triumphs over the very imprisonment in which we are involved, where we only fulfil our own possibilities and only believe in our own possibilities. . . . It is God's triumph. . . . It is a state or position in which man may very well find himself, but only with amazement, only with gratitude, in humble recognition of an accomplished fact, without any opportunity to think how it might come to pass, without possessing any need or capacity to derive it from his earlier state or to indicate the way which led from the one to the other. That earlier state was one of self-glorification and self-will. Apart from the triumph of God, it would still be his to-day. . . . He would again be forgetting or denying the triumph of God if in his new state or in the isolation, the relativizing, and the outdistancing of the old, he saw the activity of any other power than that which is the power of God in us, and which with Holy Scripture we call the power of the Holy Spirit' (*Church Dogmatics* I. 2, Part III, trans. G. T. Thomson and H. Knight [Edinburgh: T. & T. Clark, 1956], sec. 16, p. 260).

8-10 The phrase **for the sake of Christ** is now amplified and its significance developed through a series of striking phrases: **for the sake of the supreme good, the knowledge of Christ Jesus my Lord ... that I may gain Christ and be found in him ... to the end that I may come to know him and the power of his resurrection and fellowship of his sufferings, conforming myself** (or 'being conformed') **to his death.** The supreme good—that which surpasses all that life can offer—is defined, in terms most unusual for Paul, as **the knowledge of Christ Jesus my Lord** (the word rendered **knowledge** is taken as the genitive of apposition). He does not speak anywhere else of 'the knowledge of Christ', or of 'knowing Christ', but of 'the knowledge of God', and of 'knowing God'. The one exception which might be alleged is the startling negation of 2 Corinthians v. 16: 'Though we have known Christ after the flesh, yet now we know him thus no longer' (this we may reasonably take to imply a knowledge of Christ 'after the spirit').

Knowledge (*gnosis*) was one of the key words of the contemporary religion and philosophy of religion, and Paul sometimes uses it in senses which are related to that which it has in the Hellenistic theosophies, as of a *revealed* knowledge of the mystery of salvation—though never in the sense of a knowledge of Self as essentially one with the divine Self, or as the key to a mystic absorption into the divine essence, or to the freeing of the soul from its imprisonment. As a matter of fact, he does not always make it clear just what he means by *gnosis*. He assumes that the word and its connotations are familiar to his readers, and often enough, he appears to be taking it up from the usage of his readers rather than using it as a term of his own theological vocabulary. In some instances, he warns against the dangers inherent in some types of *gnosis* which have proved attractive to his Gentile converts. 'Knowledge puffs us up; love builds us up,' he writes to the Corinthians; 'if any man supposes that he has come to know something, he does not yet know as it is necessary for us to know; but if any man loves God, this man is known by him' (1 Cor. viii. 1-3). This insistence on the primacy of *love*, the superiority of love over *gnosis*, is so often repeated in his writings (e.g. 1 Cor. xiii. 2, 8; and especially the thoroughly Pauline phrase of Eph. iii. 19: 'to know the love of Christ, which excels *gnosis*'), that it is surprising to find such a note missing here. Dom J. Dupont can only explain its absence on the ground that Paul here is reverting to an inherited Jewish ideal. 'When he makes "knowledge" the supreme value of the religious life, he speaks in keeping with the ideal of *paideia* of a doctor of the Law or with the mystic aspirations of apocalyptic; his language is on the contrary specifically Christian when he puts the values of "love" above everything.' Dupont thinks that Paul was led to affirm the primacy of love in the specific circumstances of the abuses which had occurred in the church of Corinth. 'The theology of love was not born at that moment, but it was then, in open conflict with Judaic conceptions, that Paul brought out forcefully the originality of the new religion. It is remarkable that afterwards, when he writes the epistles of the Captivity, he should return to the Judaic appreciation of the values of religious knowledge' (*Gnosis: la connaissance religieuse dans les épîtres de saint Paul* [Bruges and Paris: Desclée de Brower, 1949], p. 415).

Such an explanation is not in the least satisfactory, nor is it necessary; Dom Dupont is led into it by his persuasion that Paul's use of *gnosis* is wholly rooted in Jewish conceptions of 'the knowledge of God', and reflects the connotations of the Hebrew root YD', without any influence of Hellenistic mysticism or the language of Greek philosophy.[1] But the words of the distinguished Benedictine scholar will serve to emphasize that we are faced with an exceptionally difficult problem of interpretation, and to put us on our guard against satisfying ourselves too readily with facile explanations.

First of all, it must be remarked that the transition from 'knowledge of God'—the familiar Hebrew expression—to

---

[1] Dupont's position in this respect is radically different from that of R. Bultmann, as expounded in his article *Gnosis* (*BKW*, v); see also his review of Dupont's book in *JTS*, n.s. iii (1952), pp. 10-26.

'knowledge of Christ' is by no means simple in itself. It becomes clear, as we go on to the following verses, that the idea of the knowledge of Christ is developed in ways that could not conceivably have any parallel in the idea of the knowledge of God. For **the knowledge of Christ** is associated with—we might even say, it is expounded as—knowing **the power of his resurrection and fellowship of his sufferings,** and **conforming myself to his death.** Here is a whole range of thought that goes far beyond anything that belongs to the Hebraic conception of 'the knowledge of God', and is in fact related significantly to conceptions, which can only be termed 'Hellenistic', of *mystical participation* in the accomplished experience of the Saviour. We must, therefore, agree with M. Dibelius that *gnosis* 'is used in the technical sense given it in Hellenistic mysticism' (Commentary, 3rd ed., *ad loc.*). **The knowledge of Christ** is not, for Paul, a mere Christianizing of the Hebrew 'knowledge of God': the idea of 'knowledge' has undergone a profound change, with the change of object.

None the less, even in this broadly Hellenistic and mystical context, the words *gnosis* and *ginōskō* ('knowledge' and 'know') retain religious and moral overtones of the greatest importance, carried over from the Hebraic usage. Let us turn, for instance, to the language of Hosea, as it has been expounded by Sir George Adam Smith. 'Using the word *knowledge*, in the passive sense characteristic of his language, not so much the acquisition as the impression of facts, an impression which masters not only a man's thoughts but his heart and will, Hosea describes the *knowledge of God* as feeling, character, and conscience. Again and again he makes it parallel to loyalty, repentance, love and service. Again and again he emphasizes that it comes from God Himself. . . . Hosea presents the knowledge of the Most High, not as something which man finds out for himself, but something which comes down on him from above'(*The Book of the Twelve Prophets*, vol. i, in 'The Expositor's Bible' [London: Hodder & Stoughton, 1905], p. 325). For Paul, likewise, the knowledge of Christ is 'an impression which masters not only a man's thoughts but his heart and will'; it involves 'loyalty, repentance, love and service', and it is the response of faith to revelation. Just as there are elements in our passage which go beyond the range of anything in the Old Testament conceptions of the knowledge of God; so we have here elements which have no parallel in the language or thought of Hellenistic mysticism. As in so many other instances, we find Paul making a new, creative fusion of the Hellenic with the Hebraic, which issues in a distinctively *Christian* synthesis far richer than either, though it is the heir of both.

Next, it must be emphasized that knowledge—**the knowledge of Christ**—is not here used in the sense of a Christian virtue, which might be arranged in a list of virtues or 'spiritual gifts' along with others, with gradations of value. **The knowledge of Christ** is here represented as the whole substance of the Christian life. The Apostle is not talking about *la connaissance religieuse* as a mode of spiritual experience, but about his own personal relationship with Christ under all its modes. And though he does not use the word *agapē* ('love') in the passage, it is evident in every word that this relationship is essentially a relationship of love; **the knowledge of Christ** is the knowledge of one who loves and knows himself beloved. Here and here alone in his writings do we find the intensely personal **Christ Jesus my Lord;** and it would be a dull reader indeed who did not mark the warm and deep devotion which breathes through every phrase.

For whose sake I forfeited everything. The verb is actually a passive, and could be rendered literally 'I was mulcted' (of all my possessions); it is the cognate of the noun rendered **loss.** Perhaps it is meant to have its full force; the Apostle may be thinking concretely of the penalties inflicted upon him by the Jewish authorities. We are not acquainted with the particulars; he may well have been disowned by his family and disinherited, or had property confiscated, and been deprived of all his rights in the national community of Judaism. More probably, he is thinking in more general terms, of the fact that allegiance to Christ has involved the renunciation of all that he formerly prized; primarily, the high status which he had held in Judaism (vv. 5-6, above). In a like vein, he writes to the Galatians: 'Far be it from me to glory except in the cross of our Lord Jesus Christ, through whom a world has been crucified to me and I to a world' (Gal. vi. 14; cf. Burton's note: 'Paul's world . . . was that of Israelitish descent, circumcision, the rank and dignity of a Pharisee, the righteousness that is in law, touching which he was blameless').

Rubbish—a strong word, which may mean 'street-sweepings', or 'the refuse of the table', or even 'excrement' (whence AV 'dung'). He has no regrets, for he attaches no value whatever to what he has renounced.

That I may gain Christ—the verb is the cognate of the noun rendered **gain** above (v. 7). It is probably best to take the clause as dependent upon the two verbs in the present tense: **I count everything as loss . . . I count it all rubbish, that I may gain Christ.** That is, he is anticipating the thought which he is going to stress from verse 12 on, that the goal is still to be reached. There is undoubtedly a sense in which he might say: 'I forfeited everything . . . that I might win Christ', with the implication that he has won Christ, and counted the world well lost for this; but it is more in keeping with the tenor of the whole passage that he should be speaking of the dynamic of his life; not of what the past has given, but of his present aspirations and his future hope.

9   **Be found in him.** Some good commentators take this as a reference to the final judgment, or to his state at death (so explicitly James Moffatt: 'be found at death in him'). There is, however, no indication that Paul is thinking of any particular moment, any more than in the expression of his desire that he **may win Christ.** The two expressions are parallel, and both bear upon his aspirations for the whole course of his life, without specific pointing towards its final outcome. 'The entire line of thought refers to union with Christ in this life' (Vincent, *ad loc.*). As in the French *se trouver*, the notion of 'finding' has virtually disappeared; the verb means little more than 'be in fact' (cf. Gal. ii. 17: 'But if while we are seeking to be justified in Christ, we ourselves also were found to be sinners . . .'; with Burton's note: 'It is clear from N.T. examples that *heurethēn* in particular had the sense "prove to be", "turn out to be", almost "to become", without special thought of the discovery of the fact' [*Galatians*, I.C.C., p. 125]). **In him**—united with Christ in the life which he imparts to and shares with all his followers. Paul speaks frequently of the Christian believer as

being 'in Christ'; he can likewise speak of Christ as 'in me' or 'in you' (e.g. Rom. viii. 10; Gal. ii. 20). The life **in Christ** is never conceived as a continuance of the former life under new conditions, but as a new life which is nothing else than the heavenly and divine life of the risen Christ himself. The old life is not simply purged of its evil aspects; even that which is best and highest in it has no value for the life in Christ; its **gain** is counted **loss;** it is given up to death, to crucifixion with Christ. 'I am crucified with Christ', writes the Apostle, 'It is no longer I that live, but Christ lives in me' (Gal. ii. 19). To **win Christ and be found in him** thus means the renunciation of the former life, not only in respect of its sins, but in respect of its very goodness—anything in it that could be called **righteousness,** as he will now go on to say.

Not having a righteousness of my own . . . but the righteousness which proceeds from God. In this one verse, Paul recalls his great fundamental doctrine of justification by faith, which is the central theme of his epistle to the Romans and the core of his argument in the epistle to the Galatians. Here the doctrine is not expounded; it is assumed that the readers will know without further explanation all that it involves. If we did not possess Romans and Galatians, we should find his words all but incomprehensible: It is evident that behind his words about **the knowledge of Christ** there lies an equally wide and well-developed body of doctrine, but we have nothing comparable to Romans and Galatians to aid us in arriving at its fuller understanding.

ADDITIONAL NOTE: On 'Righteousness' and 'Justify' in the Usage of Paul.

Few words in the Pauline vocabulary offer as great difficulty as δικαιοσύνη ('righteousness') and its cognates, especially the verb δικαιόω ('justify'). The noun is rendered in Latin by *justitia* (here and in Romans and Galatians), so that Roman Catholic versions in English, and Roman Catholic commentators, use the word 'justice'; and this unquestionably conveys a different sense to English ears than our familiar rendering 'righteousness'. This is the word used by Plato in the *Republic*, which might even be described as an enquiry into the meaning

of 'justice', and it has come down through the vocabulary of
moral philosophy as one of the four cardinal virtues. But the
background of Paul's usage is not to be found, or at least it is
only partly to be found, in moral philosophy; it must be traced
to the Septuagint, and beyond that to the Hebraic vocabulary
which lies behind the Septuagint, to the Hebrew conception of
'righteousness', which begins from the conception of God as
righteous and the righteousness of God. That is to say, the
conception is primarily *religious*, as in Greek it is not; and its
moral content derives from and rests upon the notion of a right
relationship with God, obedient conformity to the Law of God,
the kind of character and conduct that will be approved by God
the righteous Judge.

For the Judaism in which Paul was reared, **righteousness**
for man consisted in scrupulous fulfilment of the requirements
of the Law of God; and by the terms of that system of obser-
vances, he was able to claim that he was **blameless** (v. 6). Yet,
as we have observed, this was by the terms of a system which
attached no blame to the persecution of the church. And in a
profounder sense, Paul had come to realize that it was always
beyond the power of man to fulfil the requirements of the Law,
for there was no *power* in the Law to enable him to overcome
the sinful impulses and irrational desires of his nature as man.
The Law gave him the knowledge of sin; he could acknowledge
that it was holy and just and good; but he found himself
involved in an endless inward conflict in which he could not win
the victory. 'I delight in the law of God in my inward self; but
I observe in my members another law which keeps campaigning
against the law that my mind approves, and making me a
captive' (Rom. vi. 7-25). He found himself a slave, 'sold into
slavery under sin' (v. 14), and wholly incapable of setting himself free; and he cried in despair: 'Wretched man that I am!
Who will rescue me from this body of death?' (v. 24). Out of
his own experience of failure in the moral struggle, he learned
that **the righteousness which rests on the Law,** or **the kind
of righteousness which issues from Law**—anything that he
could proudly claim as **a righteousness of my own**—could
not set him in the right before God. He, the most devout of
Pharisees, was guilty before God, like all the world; and there

was no justification to be achieved through the works of the Law (Rom. iii. 20).

In the Gospel he has learned of another kind of righteousness—**the righteousness which is given through faith in Christ;** or, as he puts it more fully, **the righteousness which proceeds from God and is accorded to faith.** Here we must again turn to the fuller exposition which he has left us in his epistle to the Romans. He tells us that the Gospel is 'God's power put forth to bring salvation to every one who has faith. ... For in it God's righteousness is revealed, from faith to faith, as it is written, "He who is righteous through faith shall live"' (Rom. i. 16-17). And a little further on he develops the thought more fully: 'Now, *apart from Law*, God's righteousness is revealed ... God's righteousness, through faith in Jesus Christ, for all who believe . . . being justified freely, by his grace, through the redemption that is in Christ Jesus' (Rom. iii. 21-24). God has done what the Law could not do, in sending his Son (Rom. viii. 3). The only righteousness which will avail for Paul is 'God's righteousness', which is made known in Christ and **is accorded to faith,** not as a reward for the deserving, but as a free gift to the undeserving—the forgiveness of sins, the grant of access to the divine Presence ('this grace wherein we stand' —Rom. v. 1) and the assured hope of life eternal.

For **the righteousness which proceeds from God** is not to be understood in simply moral terms; Paul is not simply saying, or hoping, that he is a better, a more upright, more 'righteous' man than he was before. There is no thought here of an accumulated goodness, or of an increasing moral improvement, which a man can achieve by 'faith' if he only abandons the attempt to achieve it through 'the works of the Law'. **Faith in Christ** is not another kind of virtue; else it too would become **a righteousness of my own. Faith** for Paul is the necessary correlative of *grace*; see the striking phrase of Rom. iii. 16: 'For this reason it is of faith, that it may be based upon grace'. It is not a claim upon God, but a confession of total dependence upon God, and a continual recognition of helplessness to do anything of ourselves to better our condition before God; and a continual willingness to receive as a gift from God that which we can by no means procure or help to procure for ourselves. **The righteousness which proceeds from God and is accorded to faith,** accordingly, is not a higher kind of moral attainment, but is basically a *right relationship* with God, which God himself creates through Christ, and opens freely to all who believe in Christ. It is always and only the gift of God, and not in any degree the achievement of man.

The great difficulty in the way of understanding Paul's language about *righteousness* lies just in this, that he uses the word in two different senses. When he speaks of **a righteousness of my own—the righteousness which rests on the Law,** or **the kind of righteousness which issues from Law** —it means an approved conduct and character, a level of moral achievement which God as the Judge of men will approve. But when he speaks of **the righteousness which proceeds from God and is accorded to faith,** it no longer means a level of moral achievement, or a conduct and character improved to the point where it meets God's approval. In this context, the righteousness which Paul has is no longer a matter of his own character and conduct at all, even as relatively 'better' than in his life as a scrupulous, Law-revering Pharisee. He is not laying claim to some kind of moral superiority which God has given him, which he could not achieve by the most rigorous application of a Pharisaic discipline of conformity to Law. **The righteousness which proceeds from God** rests upon the thought that God has 'justified' him; that is to say, has pronounced him righteous, has reckoned to him a righteousness which he does not possess and has not imputed to him the trespasses which he has committed; and he can illustrate his meaning by citing the Psalm (xxxii. 1, 2): 'Blessed are those whose iniquities are forgiven and whose sins are covered; blessed is the man whose sin the Lord will not reckon against him' (Rom. iv. 7-8; cf. also vv. 4-6). We are bound to feel, in fact, that **righteousness** has here had forced upon it a meaning which is not really proper to it; in this context, the meaning which is required would be given better by the word 'forgiveness'. **The righteousness which proceeds from God and is accorded to faith** is, basically and primarily, the forgiveness of sins.

If Paul retains the word **righteousness** in this unnatural sense which he forces upon it, it is probably in some degree an unconscious carry-over from the vocabulary of his earlier religious training and outlook into a realm in which it is no longer at home. 'Forensic' language cannot be used without strain in the context of divine dealings with man which are expressly put under the rubric 'apart from Law' (Rom. iii. 21). Yet this is not the whole story. **Righteousness** still carries connotations which go well beyond the meaning of 'forgiveness'. For one thing, the word **righteousness** here preserves for Paul the eschatological moment of his thinking; the ever-present sense that the forgiveness which God now bestows upon the sinner who has faith in Christ is an anticipation of the verdict which he will deliver upon him at the day of judgment. On this, see the notes of C. K. Barrett, *Romans*, pp. 74 ff., 87 ff. Thus he can speak now of justification as granted already, and write: 'Since we have been justified on the basis of faith, let us have peace with God' (Rom. v. 1); and now (much less frequently), he can speak of it as an object of hope: 'We by the Spirit, by faith, wait for the hope of righteousness' (Gal. v. 5). And there is this further element, that **righteousness** in Paul's usage retains also the sense of 'victory' which belongs to the Hebrew words *tsedeq* and *ts'daqah*, especially in the exultant language of the Second Isaiah. God's 'righteousness' is here the victorious power which ensures the triumph of good over evil and brings in the kingdom of peace on earth. So **the righteousness which proceeds from God and is accorded to faith** is not alone the forgiveness of sins, but is also the power which God imparts to the believer, which 'takes command of the whole of life as the victor over unrighteousness and sin' (G. Schenck, *BKW*, iv, 'Righteousness', p. 53). This victory is also eschatologically conceived; that is, it is an anticipation in life of God's final and total victory; and for that reason, it is never more than partial under the conditions of the present age.

It might be added that the word **righteousness** retains the thought, undoubtedly of primary significance to Paul, that the forgiveness of sins does not impair the justice of God in judging the world; in 'the act of redemption which he performed in Christ Jesus', God has so acted as 'to show forth and vindicate his righteousness in this present time, so that he might both be righteous himself, and justify the man who relies on faith in Jesus' (Rom. iii. 24, 26, Barrett).

10   The thought of **the knowledge of Christ,** introduced in v. 8 as **the supreme good** for which Paul has **forfeited everything,** is now taken up and developed in terms of *power* and *fellowship*, experienced through participation with Christ in his sufferings and death and in his resurrection. The Apostle tells us that his whole life is so ordered **to the end that I may come to know him and the power of his resurrection and fellowship of his sufferings, conforming myself to his death.** Clearly the knowledge of which he here speaks is a knowledge gained through personal experience; and that experience is conceived in the first instance *mystically*. **The power of his resurrection** is the life-giving power of God, the power which he manifested in raising Christ from the dead, and which he now manifests in the new life which the Christian receives from the risen Christ and shares with him. To **know** . . . this **power** is to experience its effects in one's own life. If we now turn again to other writings of Paul for more light upon his meaning, we shall find that in his letter to the Romans he teaches that this new life begins in baptism, which symbolizes, and mystically effects, the participation of the Christian with Christ in death and resurrection (Rom. vi. 3-5). The administration of the sacrament marks the end of the old life, which was enslaved to sin and doomed to perish; and the entrance upon the new life of faith and obedience to the truth, which has its fruit in holiness and its issue in life eternal (Rom. vi. 22).

The most striking feature of the Apostle's thought here lies in the conception of this knowledge as something to be acquired, as the object which he pursues with the entire dedication of all that he has and is. Here we must ask the reader to give himself the trouble of following a brief explanation of the Greek syntax. The final clause, which has been rendered **to the end that I may come to know,** is expressed in Greek by the aorist infinitive with the genitive of the article (τοῦ γνῶναι). The aorist has what is styled 'punctiliar' action; this means that it sums up the action of the verb at a point—it may be the point at which it commences (*ingressive*) or the point at which it is completed (*effective*), or it may envisage the action in its entirety, as having taken place (*constative*). The main point is that it cannot represent action as progressive. (See J. H. Moulton, *Prolegomena*, chap. vi, pp. 109 ff.). The emphasis in the phrase, accordingly, is not on a gradual growth in knowledge, but on its final attainment, which must await **the resurrection of the dead** (v. 11). Again we perceive the strongly eschatological orientation of the Apostle's thought; and we shall particularly have in mind the words from his great hymn of Love: 'Now we see through a mirror, in a riddle; but then, face to face; now I know in part, but then shall I know as I also have been known' (1 Cor. xiii. 12). He knows Christ now, and his knowledge of Christ deepens with the years of service and of suffering in his cause; but the partial knowledge which he has attained and is attaining only intensifies his longing for the fulness of knowledge that he anticipates in 'the Day of Christ Jesus' (i. 6, 10), when he will come to know Christ as Christ knows him.

The power . . . and fellowship. In the true Greek text, the two nouns are linked closely together by the use of the one article for both; and the participial phrase **conforming myself to his death** is explanatory of both. The mystical participation with Christ in his death which was effected in baptism is the condition of sharing in the divine power of his risen life, and it is impossible to share in that life without a share of his sufferings. But here the thought is more than mystical; the reality of the mystical experience is unfolded and exhibited in the concrete matter-of-fact experience of the outward life. **Fellowship of his sufferings** means more than the mystical self-identification with the suffering Christ; it involves the thought that the sufferings endured in his own person by the Apostle (who here becomes the representative type of the Christian believer) are all of a part with the sufferings which Christ endured; and thus a deeper bond of fellowship with Christ is woven through the sufferings which are inflicted upon his follower. In the mystical unity with Christ which was inaugurated in baptism, the Christian was made one with Christ in his sufferings and death and in his triumph over death; in the sufferings of his faithful follower, Christ makes himself one with the sufferer, so that our sufferings become his sufferings, and the Apostle can say again, 'I fill up the deficiencies of the afflictions of Christ in my flesh for the sake of his body, which is the Church' (Col. i. 24). This is that **fellowship of his sufferings** which the Apostle longs **to know.**

Conforming myself to his death. The unity with Christ in his death is elsewhere expressed by Paul in the *perfect*, as of something accomplished which has become the settled condition of his existence. 'I have been crucified with Christ' (Gal. ii. 19); or, perhaps better 'I am crucified with Christ'. In that phrase, the thought bears upon the state of the Apostle considered as the resultant of the climactic experience of his baptism, when he 'died to sin' (Rom. vi. 2) and to the Law (Rom. vii. 6). Just as he can say 'Christ died', or 'Christ was crucified', and can also speak of 'Christ crucified' (in the perfect—1 Cor. i. 23; ii. 2), as if the crucifixion were conceived not solely as an event of the past, but also as in some sense the significant condition of existence of the risen Christ; so he can speak of his identification with Christ in death both in terms of the decisive past event, when he 'died', and in terms of the resultant existence in which he 'is crucified' with Christ. In the phrase before us, the thought is viewed under still a third aspect, as a progressive experience. The present participle **conforming myself** suggests a continual striving for unity with Christ in his death, the daily mortification of everything in him that is not Christ. The mystical union with Christ which was initiated in baptism is confirmed and deepened through the daily quest for a more and more complete identification with him in his dying to the life of this world and in his risen life over which death has no more dominion. Here again the thought of the Apostle is not solely mystical; the hazards and batterings to which he is subjected in his work for Christ are the concrete external means by which he is being conformed to Christ's death. His thought seems to be given a parallel expression, somewhat more comprehensively, in 2 Cor. iv. 7 ff., especially in verses 10 and 11: 'Always bearing about in our bodies the dying of Jesus, in order that the life of Jesus also may be manifested in our bodies. For we who are living are always being delivered up to death for the sake of Jesus, in order that the life of Jesus may be manifested in our mortal flesh . . . (v. 14), for we know that he who raised the Lord Jesus will also raise us with Jesus and will cause us to stand in his presence with you.'

If only I may attain to the resurrection from the dead. 11 Here again Paul links the acceptance of identification with Christ in his death to the hope of sharing his resurrection. And again we must observe the double focus of his thought: the mystical participation in the life of the risen Christ, which is his here and now ('To me to live is Christ'—i. 21; and 'It is no longer I that live, but Christ lives in me'—Gal. ii. 20) is crowned and brought to its consummation by **the resurrection from the dead.** This element of hope is fundamental to all his thinking. The presence of God's Spirit in us is to him a glorious reality; yet it is no more than the earnest of the inheritance (Eph. i. 14; taking up the phrases of 2 Cor. i. 22 and v. 5), and the manifestation of a life which will not reach its fulness until it receives expression in a 'body' fitted for its habitation as these mortal and corruptible bodies can never be. So he assures the Romans that 'if the Spirit of him who raised Jesus from the dead dwells in you, then he who raised Christ Jesus from the dead will also make alive your mortal bodies through his Spirit that dwells in you' (Rom. viii. 11). Death, the last enemy, will not be destroyed until 'this corruptible puts on (is clothed with) incorruption, and this mortal puts on immortality' (1 Cor. xv. 54).

ADDITIONAL NOTE. On the Hope of Resurrection.

There is probably no area of Paul's teaching in which we find it harder to follow the lines of his thought. Our own notions of the life of the world to come, usually ill-defined and vague, make little room for any kind of permanence of the body. Our minds are dominated, or at least profoundly affected, by our Greek (essentially Platonic) inheritance, so that we think of immortality as 'the immortality of the soul'; and whatever difficulty we may have in defining 'soul', we still feel that there is some essential part of our personality which alone is capable of immortality, and that part does not include the body. Paul, unlike us, was affected by Greek notions only in a secondary way. His inheritance was Hebraic, and the Hebrew thought instinctively of the person as a whole; for him, the body was a valid expression of the whole person, not a more or less indifferent frame for the soul. Paul was constitutionally incapable of thinking of life eternal in terms of a 'soul' existing in some disembodied state. In one passage, he seems to refer to such an idea, which he had no doubt encountered in the Greek world, only to reject it with a kind of horror. 'We know', he writes, 'that if our earthly house in which we dwell be dissolved, we have a habitation given by God, not made by hands, eternal, in the heavens. For indeed in this dwelling we groan, longing to put on our dwelling-place that is from heaven, if only having put it on we may not be found naked. For we who are in this dwelling groan under our burden: it is not that we wish to be unclothed, but to put on further clothing, to the end that our mortality may be swallowed up by life' (2 Cor. v. 1-4). Strange words to our ears, and hard to comprehend; but it does emerge clearly from them that he abhors the notion of a soul left naked, and thinks of the conditions of the future life wholly in terms of addition, not of subtraction; of something divine and heavenly added, not in terms of something earthly and perishable being cast aside. He thinks of the earthly, the perishable, the mortal, as being transformed into something infinitely higher and more glorious, not of its being discarded. A 'spiritual' resurrection would to him be no resurrection at all; a disembodied existence would be no better than the shadowy and unsubstantial existence of a shade. He is therefore bound to express his hope of immortality in terms of attaining **to the resurrection from the dead.** Even the higher blessedness into which he expects to enter at death ('to die is gain . . . to move on and to be with Christ . . . that is far and away the better'—i. 21, 23; cf. also 2 Cor. v. 6-8, especially the words, 'We are of good courage and would choose rather to depart from the body and to take up our abode with the Lord') still falls short of the fulfilment which he awaits at the coming of the Lord in glory and the resurrection from the dead. Then, as he will tell us in a following passage (iii. 21), the Lord **will refashion our body of lowliness to share the form of his body of glory.** Compare also 1 Corinthians xv. 51 ff. Then only will God **complete the good work which he has begun** in us (i. 6).

We may add here a few sentences from a remarkable essay of Oscar Cullmann. 'How ironical that the Christian church is constantly reproached with concentrating all its interest on the selfish happiness of the individual in the world beyond! To imagine that such a caricature does justice not only to Christianity but to the New Testament itself is to display total ignorance, since, unlike the belief in the immortality of the soul professed by Greek philosophy, the biblical hope of resurrection sees the destiny of the individual merely as a consequence flowing from the total work of Christ. That is why the resurrection of our "mortal bodies" (Rom. viii. 11) will only take place at the end of time: individual death will not be followed by an immediate escape from time. . . . It would be a distortion of the New Testament conception of time to say: Those who have died in Christ are already living outside time and are already participating in all that the Church expects for the end of the world, that is, the resurrection of the body and the putting on of the σῶμα πνευματικόν, which really depends on the return of Christ to earth and the recreation of matter itself.' *The Early Church*, Essay VII, 'The Return of Christ', pp. 148 ff.).

Before we go on, a word must be added about the unusual 11 form of the phrase which Paul uses here (and only here)—**the resurrection from the dead** τὴν ἐξανάστασιν τὴν ἐκ τῶν νεκρῶν; elsewhere, it is always, 'the resurrection of the dead'— [ἡ] ἀνάστασις [τῶν] νεκρῶν. The preposition ἐκ **(from)** is actually used twice; once before τῶν νεκρῶν **(the dead),** and once in composition with the governing noun. The only comparable expression in the New Testament writings is found in Luke xx. 35: 'Those who are counted worthy to attain that age (the age of the Kingdom) and the resurrection from the dead' (again, ἐκ νεκρῶν). In both passages, there is clearly involved a distinction between the resurrection of those who 'are counted worthy', and the masses of the dead who have no part in the age to come. Paul, that is to say, is not thinking of a 'general resurrection' in which all will have part, regardless of their belief or unbelief, good or evil; but of resurrection in the sense of the final attainment of the blessedness which is promised to the faithful followers of Christ. *This* resurrection is to take place at the Parousia of the Lord; cf. 1 Thessalonians iv. 16: 'For the Lord himself . . . shall descend from heaven, and the dead in Christ shall rise first; then we which are alive . . . shall be caught up along with them in clouds, for our meeting with the Lord in the air; and so we shall always be with the Lord'. (I see no reason to suppose that Paul's conception had undergone any fundamental change.) See the important article of E. Fascher, 'Anastasis—Resurrectio—Auferstehung', in *ZNTW*, 40 (1941), pp. 166-229.

We might remark at this point that the late Sir Gilbert Murray's literal rendering of *anastasis nekrōn* as 'the standing up of the corpses' was altogether silly and quite unworthy of the great classical scholar. Paul was not interested in corpses, and the Christian doctrine of the resurrection of the body is not a doctrine of the re-animation of the corpse.

See also the Additional Note, 'On Paul's Expectation of the Life to Come' (at the close of Section 5, pp. 64 f.), and the notes on iii. 20-21, below.

12-14   Paul now makes use of a favourite metaphor, drawn again from the games. He speaks of his life under the figure of a race, which can be won only if the runner gives his attention wholly to reaching the goal, and throws all his energies into the effort to get to it as quickly as possible. Life eternal—**the resurrection from the dead**—is now viewed as **the prize** which will be awarded to the winner. He knows that many a race has been lost by a runner who pulls up short of the finish line, or who allows his attention to be distracted by something off the course, or even by one who looks back over his shoulder at the track behind him. The figure cannot be sustained in every respect, for in this race the victory of one does not carry with it the defeat of all the others; **the prize** is not reserved for the one who comes first to the finish line, but is awarded to all who succeed in completing the course. Elsewhere, he uses the same figure to bring home to his readers the need for self-discipline, for rigorous training and sustained well-directed effort. 'Don't you know that in the stadium all the runners take part in the race, but only one receives the prize: that is the way that you must run—to win. And everyone who competes in the games disciplines himself in every way—they, on their part, do this to win a perishable crown, but the crown for which *we* strive is imperishable' (1 Cor. ix. 24-25). The Christian must have the ambition, the persistence, the drive that makes the winner; he may not saunter or look aside. So Paul pictures his own life in Christ—a single-minded, disciplined, direct thrust for the tape. Within the picture, however, he introduces a touch that belongs to a quite different atmosphere of thought and imagination. When he sets aside any thought that he has **attained perfection,** he is no longer thinking of himself as a runner on the course, but as an initiate in a mystery-cult. This line of thinking is not developed; the expression remains as an incongruous intrusion into a figure that is otherwise coherent and vivid.

The verb ἔλαβον—**I have won;** taken up again in the 12 compounded form καταλάβω, etc. (three times—**that I may win ...I have been won ... (I do not reckon) that I have won** is used in all four places without an object; but as the Corinthians passage cited above will indicate, the object to be supplied is **the prize.** If Paul finds it necessary to say **Not that I have already won the prize or already attained perfection,** it can only be because he knows people who think that they are already made perfect. **I have attained perfection** is *their* language; he takes it over from them, only to repudiate any such attitude for himself, and to abandon it at once for his own more truly applicable metaphor of the race. If the Christian life is to be described in terms of a race in progress, obviously the notion of an attained perfection is out of place.

The verb τετελείωμαι—**I have attained perfection**— belongs to the terminology of the mysteries (τελεταί). The person initiated, or in some cults it would be the person admitted to the highest grade, was called τέλειος—*perfect.* There is no thought of *moral* perfection involved here; it is more the notion of transition to a higher order of being, effected through the operation of sacramental rites. Ritual purifications and expiatory sacrifices were often required by way of preparation, and these might on occasion be given an ethical interpretation; but the change effected is not conceived in ethical terms, but in terms of essence. Paul is alive to the danger that the salvation proclaimed in the Gospel should be wholly transposed into similar categories; he has encountered people—indeed, the

the implication is that there will be some of them among the readers to whom this fragment is addressed—who imagine that they have been admitted to the highest level of the Christian life and have no more progress to make—they **have attained perfection.** He disabuses them of this notion, not only by repudiating any such claim for himself, but by depicting the whole life of the Christian believer in dynamic terms, in terms of strenuous and unceasing progress towards a goal that is not to be reached in this world.

13   **The things that are behind**—he is not here speaking of all those inherited advantages which he now counts worthless (vv. 7-8), but of the part of the course which he has already covered, as a Christian. He does not stop to congratulate himself upon the ground already gained; he is wholly absorbed in the

14 task of covering the ground between him and **the finish line. The prize** is sometimes taken to be defined in the accompanying phrase, as itself **the high vocation to which God has called me.** This is grammatically possible (taking κλήσεως as a genitive of apposition); but the better sense seems to be that he is thinking of Christ, whom he longs to know or to gain (vv. 8, 10), as **the prize** which is offered to those whom God calls into his service. Paul is not thinking of his vocation as an Apostle, but of the **high vocation** which he shares with all Christian believers. We are all 'partners in a heavenly calling' (Heb. iii. 1); and 'the God of all grace has called us to his eternal glory in Christ' (1 Pet. v. 10). Similarly the writer of Ephesians, the earliest of all interpreters of Paul, bids us remember that we are 'called in one hope of [our] calling' (Eph. iv. 4). It is **high** in the sense that it is a call from the earthly to the heavenly. (Cf. the paraphrase of Erasmus: 'praemium immortalitatis, ad quod Deus agonotheta noster, e coelis spectans conatum nostrum, nos vocat, opitulante Christo Jesu'.

15   Paul now appears to include himself among those who may be called **perfect;** and it is possible that he is reverting to another usage of the same adjective τέλειος, as when he distinguishes between *mature* (or 'perfect') Christians and 'babes' or 'infants' (νήπιοι) who are not yet capable of receiving solid food but have to be nourished upon milk (1 Cor. ii. 6; iii. 1 f.). It is more likely, however, that he still is keeping to the language

of those who think that they **have attained perfection;** and
by a kind of oxymoron (Haupt), almost whimsically, he suggests
that in the Christian vocabulary **perfect** can only mean
'conscious that we are not perfect', and bent upon attaining a
goal that has not yet been reached. Haupt brings before us two
very pertinent quotations; one from St. John Chrysostom: 'It
is the mark of a perfect man, not to reckon himself perfect';
and one from Luther: 'The nature of a Christian does not lie
in what he has become, but in what he is becoming [*nicht im
Wordensein, sondern im Werden*], wherefore he who is a Christian
is no Christian'. **So disposed**—as Paul has described his own
outlook and attitude.

Paul does not expect that all his readers will wholly agree
with him; and he shows a remarkable tolerance of differing
judgments. He is ready to wait until God opens the minds of
the others to the truth as he has expounded it. **If you look on
things at all differently, this too God will reveal to you.**
It is striking to observe that he does not require submission to
his interpretation of the will of God; he is not content to stand
upon his apostolic authority and demand unthinking acceptance
of his teaching. Neither does he take it for granted that he can
make his point by cogent reasonings. He counts on God to
bring illumination to their minds. The revelation of divine
truth is not conveyed solely through the apostolate, nor indeed
can it be made effective by virtue of an external authority of any
kind; it requires also the enlightening of 'the eyes of the heart'
(Eph. i. 18).

The concluding phrase of verse 16 is very difficult to interpret 16
as it stands, and this difficulty has given rise to a number of
variant readings. Paul here uses the infinitive for the imperative
(στοιχεῖν—**stand in line,** or perhaps 'march in line'). To the
rather vague dative τῷ αὐτῷ—literally, 'by the same'—apparently
referring to the preceding phrase **at the point which we have
already reached**—some scribes have added the noun κανόνι
('rule'), probably by an unconscious reminiscence of Gal. vi.
16: 'As many as shall walk by this canon, or rule'. The general
thought seems to be that even though we admit differences of
insight, different levels of apprehension of the truth, we must
live by the highest that we have been able to grasp; we must not

fall back from **the point which we have already reached.**
Yet he seems to be trying to avoid the suggestion that Christians
are to be spiritual virtuosos, each pursuing his own inward
development in keeping with his individual attainments. By
his choice of the verb στοιχεῖν, which has the basic sense of
standing **in line** (as of a row of figures or letters, or the pickets
of a fence), he seeks in some degree to preserve the thought
of the unity of Christians in the contest in which all are engaged together. If it be once admitted that our perfection after
all amounts only to relative stages of imperfection, we shall
realize more clearly that we are all working towards the same
goal, and shall be ready to help one another instead of criticizing
or envying one another. But it must be admitted that the thought
is not clearly expressed, partly because the imagery of the race
here breaks down.

For an exposition of the passage (especially verses 10 to 14)
which is truly magnificent, I beg to draw attention to an article
of Jules Lebreton, which is unfortunately buried in a relatively
unknown Festschrift; viz., 'La Doctrine spirituelle du Nouveau
Testament', *Mélanges E. Podechard: études de science religieuse
offertes . . . au doyen honoraire de la Faculté de Théologie de Lyon*
(Lyon: Facultés Catholiques, 1945), pp. 175-190, pages of
sublime truth and beauty.

12. A WARNING AGAINST SELF-INDULGENCE.
iii. 17-iv. 1

**(17) Join in imitating me, brethren, and keep your eyes
fixed on those who live in this way, as you see exemplified
in us. (18) For there are many who live very differently:
I have told you of them before and now too I speak of
them with tears—they are the enemies of the cross of
Christ. (19) Their end is perdition, their god is their belly
and their glory lies in their shame; their hearts are set
on earthly things. (20) For our homeland is in heaven,
and from heaven we await a Saviour, the Lord Jesus
Christ, (21) who will refashion our body of lowliness to**

share the form of his body of glory, in keeping with the effectual action of his power even to bring all things into subjection to himself. (iv. 1) Therefore, my brethren, beloved and longed for, my joy and crown, stand firm in this way in the Lord, beloved.

The connection of this passage with that which it follows is not immediately clear. A surprising number of generally sober commentators have felt themselves obliged to link the two sections of the interpolation by identifying **the dogs, the malicious labourers,** the people of **the incision** of verse 2 with **the enemies of the cross of Christ** of v. 18. But it is surely unnatural to suppose that the zealous follower of the Jewish Law—the kind of man that Paul himself was before his conversion—is now described as one **whose god is [his] belly.** It has even been proposed that we should take this phrase as a reference to the food laws! But is it even conceivable that Paul should use such words of men who held to the dietary regulations of Judaism for no other reason than that they believed them to be ordained of God? Even more astounding is the suggestion that the phrase **their glory lies in their shame** could be a sneer at their pride in their circumcision! Paul is firm enough in his rejection of the demand that Gentile converts should be circumcised; but he never hints that anyone should be ashamed of his circumcision. On the contrary, he counsels the Corinthians not to make it a matter of any importance at all: 'Was any one at the time of his call already circumcised? Let him not seek to have the circumcision undone. Has anyone received his call while uncircumcised? Let him not be circumcised. Circumcision is nothing, and uncircumcision is nothing; all that matters is the keeping of God's commandments' (1 Cor. vii. 18-19). Or as he puts it again in writing to the Galatians: 'In Christ Jesus neither circumcision nor uncircumcision has any power, but faith acting effectively through love' (Gal. v. 6). We must insist that this is a long way from any thought that the man who is proud of being circumcised is glorying in something shameful!

We must hold, therefore, that Paul has now in view a quite different kind of danger for the church. In the former section, he has spoken of the danger of legalism, and of a righteousness based on Law; now he turns to the danger of antinomianism, the casting aside of all restraints, the degeneration of freedom into license. The connection between the two sections is obscured by the fact that Paul has not here spoken of the Christian life in terms of freedom; but in the back of his mind, there is the unexpressed sense that 'Christ has set us free' (Gal. v. 1); that 'now we are done with the law since we died to that by which we were held fast' (Rom. vii. 6, Barrett). And he knows that this new freedom in Christ has been perversely interpreted by some into an excuse for all manner of self-indulgence. Thus he has no sooner urged the Galatians to 'stand fast' in their Christian freedom, and not to put their necks again under the yoke of slavery to Law (Gal. v. 1), than he is impelled to warn them against the opposite error, of imagining that freedom from Law means license to sin with impunity. 'You were called for freedom, brethren; only do not make your freedom a vantage-point for indulgence of the flesh; but through love be slaves one of another' (Gal. v. 13). It is this unspoken correlate of freedom that links the thought of the two sections. The warning against a legalism that would destroy the true and proper freedom of the Christian believer is coupled with a warning against the perverse abuse of freedom which makes a mockery of the gospel and turns its advocates into **the enemies of the cross of Christ.**

It is of more than passing interest to note that Erasmus of Rotterdam anticipated some of our modern commentators (among whom we must include Karl Barth and Maurice Goguel) in identifying **the enemies of the cross of Christ** of this passage with **the dogs** of verse 2. He suggests that from the beginning of the chapter, Paul is warning his readers against 'semi-Christians', who are far more dangerous to the faith than the most hostile pagans; for 'sic Christum praedicant, ut Iudaismum interim admisceant. Hac de re vos pro mea sollicitudine frequenter admonui, sed tamen non gravabor eadem inculcare litteris, quo magis sitis in tuto. . . . Pro vera pietate docent Iudaicas observatiunculas, circumcisionem praeputii, ciborum delectum, discrimina dierum, ut his aliis oneratis ipsi interim regnant et suaviter vivant, perinde quasi post hanc vitam non exspectent aliam.'

Join in imitating me—first of all, in the approach to life 17 which has just been described (vv. 7-14); not seeking to parade **a righteousness of [their] own,** but to **gain Christ and be found in him,** with **the righteousness which proceeds from God and is accorded to faith;** counting **everything as loss for the sake of . . . the knowledge of Christ Jesus;** not reckoning the race as won, but speeding on to the tape, to win the prize of their calling. But more generally, Paul offers himself and those who live as he does, as a pattern of conduct, of the kind of life that befits those who profess to believe in Christ. We must keep in mind the peculiar difficulties of a minority who have adopted a new faith. They are deprived of the supports of the social system; and this of itself can lead to a moral collapse—'ethics' are so much a matter of convention, of conformity to what 'is done' or 'not done' in the community at large. The accepted standards of the pagan community are no longer a sufficient guide for those who have been 'redeemed from the aimless way of life which was inherited from their ancestors' (1 Pet. i. 18). The new life cannot be wholly set forth by precept; it must be embodied in the lives of Christ's ministers. Paul is deeply conscious of his responsibility to give his converts an example of holy Christian living. 'You are our witnesses, and God also,' he writes to the Thessalonians, 'how holily and uprightly and blamelessly we behaved ourselves towards you who believe' (1 Thess. ii. 10).

Those who live in this way—the verb used here means literally 'walk'; it reflects the Hebrew *halakh*, widely used of the moral and spiritual life; as, for instance, in Psalm cxix. 1-3: 'Blessed are the undefiled in the way, who walk in the way of the Lord. . . . They also do no iniquity: they walk in his ways.' It cannot be interpreted as meaning 'to hold such and such an attitude'; it must be given the sense of 'live' in terms of moral behaviour.

There are many who live very differently (the words 18 **very differently** are supplied, to complete the sense). It is not evident that such were to be found at Philippi (or among the community to which the fragment is addressed, if it be not Philippi). The Apostle speaks out of his knowledge, distressing him as it does, of the sensuality of some who yet claim to be followers of Christ. For there is no doubt that he is speaking of professing Christians; he would not weep over the licentious conduct of outright pagans, or call the voluptuaries among them in any special sense **the enemies of the cross of Christ.** The words must refer to people who make a virtue of their vicious behaviour; perhaps they are akin to those who say: 'We have fellowship with him', while they 'walk in darkness' (1 John i. 6), or with those who say: 'Let us do evil, that good may come', or 'Let us continue in sin, that grace may abound' (Rom. iii. 8; vi. 1).

19   **Their god is their belly**—there is no need to go beyond the obvious meaning; these are people who are interested chiefly in the pleasures of the table—if not gluttons or drunkards, they are gourmets, with no thought of anything else in life. **Their glory lies in their shame**—quite simply, they boast of conduct that ought to be regarded as shameful. **Their hearts are set on earthly things**—despite their profession of belief in Christ and his gospel, they have no thought of heavenly things. We have here almost the exact contrary of the Christian outlook, as Paul puts it before the Colossians: 'If you were raised with Christ, seek the things that are above, . . . set your hearts on the things that are above, not on the things that are upon the earth' (Col. iii. 1, 3).

20   **For our homeland is in heaven.** There is an ellipsis here, as often occurs in the use of γάρ—**for.** The unspoken thought is: 'Such conduct is not fitting in a Christian believer, **for** . . .' We cannot have our **hearts set on earthly things, for** earth to us is alien territory. **Homeland**—the word (πολίτευμα) may mean 'constitution', or 'political community'. It has been fancied that Paul is choosing a figure particularly apt for Philippi, a Roman colony, conscious of its ties with Rome and the reflection of Roman institutions in its own communal life; thus he would be thinking of the Christians as 'a colony of heaven' (Moffatt), an outpost governed by the laws of the homeland and attached to it by the deepest sentiments of loyalty. Apart from this particular point, which must be regarded as valid if the fragment be addressed to Philippi, Paul is using a theme which is often sounded in the early literature of the church. Paul himself speaks of 'the Jerusalem which is above

... which is the mother of us all' (Gal. iv. 26); the author of Hebrews tells of the men of faith, who 'confessed that they were strangers and pilgrims upon earth', and who 'desire a better country, that is an heavenly' (Heb. xi. 13, 16); in First Peter, Christians are addressed as 'chosen sojourners of the Dispersion', and are charged as 'foreigners and sojourners' to abstain from gratifying 'the fleshy desires which make war against the soul' (1 Pet. i. 1; ii. 11). In the second century, the thought is developed in the anonymous *Epistle to Diognetus*: 'Christians ... inhabit the lands of their birth, but as temporary residents thereof; they take their share of responsibilities as citizens, and endure all disabilities as aliens. Every foreign land is native to them, and every native land, foreign territory. . . . They pass their days upon earth, but they hold citizenship in heaven.'

From heaven we await a Saviour. It is surprising to note that this is the only time that we find Paul using the title **Saviour,** in referring to Jesus; and it is significant that in this one occurrence the title is given in connection with the final deliverance which the Lord is to accomplish at his coming. For in Paul's vocabulary, 'salvation' is not used of the condition into which the believer has been brought now, in this life, through his incorporation into Christ; but of the condition into which he will be brought at the Parousia. He has been 'justified', but he has not yet been 'saved'. Paul can indeed speak of salvation as a process, but never as an accomplished fact. He can say, for instance, that 'the word of the Cross is folly to those who are perishing, but to us who are being saved it is God's power' (1 Cor. i. 18). But far more often he speaks of it wholly in terms of the future hope. Thus he can set it over against justification, by way of contrast between what has been done in us by the action of God in Christ, and what remains to be done—though to be sure, the one is the assurance of the other. 'Since then we have now been justified at the cost of his blood, much more shall we be saved through him from God's wrath; for if when we were enemies we were reconciled to God through the death of his Son, much more, now that we have been reconciled, shall we be saved by his life' (Rom. v. 9-10, Barrett). The work of Christ as **Saviour,** then, remains to be accomplished. We *await* his coming **from heaven** in his role of **Saviour.**

It is to be noticed, further, that Paul speaks of our expectation of the future, not in terms of our 'going to heaven', but in terms of Christ's coming **from heaven.** That is to say, he is not thinking of the change that comes to the individual Christian believer at death, when he will 'move on and be with Christ, which is far and away the better' (i. 23); but of the consummation which will mark the final triumph of Christ, 'the times of restitution of all things' (Acts iii. 21), when 'the creation itself also shall be liberated from the corrupting bondage in which it lies, to attain the freedom which springs from the glory of the children of God' (Rom. viii. 21, Barrett). The salvation for which the Christian hopes is not truly conceived in terms of the escape of 'the soul' from 'the burden of the flesh', but in terms of the participation of the whole person in the regeneration of God's entire creation. The bliss of the redeemed, accordingly, in the Apostle's thought, is not complete in the state into which he enters at death, since he still awaits 'the redemption of the body' (Rom. viii. 23) and the establishment of God's kingdom upon earth, for which he daily prays: 'Thy kingdom come; thy will be done in earth, as it is in heaven'. See also the remarkable article of P. Benoît, '"Nous gémissons, attendant la délivrance de notre corps" (Rom. viii. 23)', in *RSR*, 39 (1951–52), pp. 267-278.

21   At his coming, the Saviour **will refashion our body of lowliness to share the form of his body of glory.** These words alone would suffice to show that Paul does not think of his eternal blessedness in terms of the separation of the soul from the body. Salvation in his thinking is not the survival of 'the soul', but the fulness of life of the whole person. So he can write to the Thessalonians, 'May the God of peace consecrate you in your wholeness [ὁλοτελεῖς], and may your spirit and soul and body be kept in wholeness [ὁλόκληρον], blameless, at the coming of our Lord Jesus Christ' (1 Thess. v. 23). The thought may be illustrated further by his doctrine of the resurrection as he expounds it in 1 Corinthians xv. He does not think of the body of flesh as surviving, or as being restored, to enter into the life eternal. On the contrary, he teaches explicitly

that 'flesh and blood cannot inherit the kingdom of God, neither doth corruption inherit incorruption . . . but this corruptible must put on incorruption, and this mortal must put on immortality' (vv. 50, 53). Yet in some sense, 'the dead shall be raised'—not in the sense that the body laid in the tomb emerges from it, for 'that which thou sowest, thou sowest not the body that shall be, but God giveth it a body as it hath pleased him' (vv. 37-38). The nature of the resurrection-body he does not attempt to describe, except in contrast with the body that is buried. 'It is sown in corruption; it is raised in incorruption: It is sown in dishonour; it is raised in glory: It is sown in weakness; it is raised in power: it is sown a natural body [σῶμα ψυχικόν]; it is raised a spiritual body [σῶμα πνευματικόν]' (vv. 42-44). A 'spiritual body' seems to be a contradiction in terms; certainly to any Greek thinker, it would have been a notion exceedingly difficult to grasp, except that we must not forget that for a Greek 'spirit' is not 'immaterial', but is conceived rather as made of a subtler kind of matter (the Stoic *pneuma*, for instance, is also *fire*, one of the four 'elements' of the universe). But it is impossible for Paul to think of the body as indifferent, as a mere garment that can be cast aside; for 'the body is . . . for the Lord, and the Lord for the body'; 'your bodies are the members of Christ'; and 'your body is the temple of the Holy Ghost which is in you, which ye have of God' (1 Cor. vi. 13, 15, 19); and Paul can charge us solemnly: 'by the mercies of God, that [we] present [our] bodies a living sacrifice, holy, acceptable unto God' (Rom. xii. 1). In his conception, therefore, the work of salvation is not complete until 'he that raised up Christ from the dead shall also quicken your mortal bodies by his Spirit that dwelleth in you' (Rom. viii. 11).

The doctrine is by no means unambiguous, for the Apostle's language seems now to convey the thought of some kind of continuity between the body which we now bear, and the body that shall be; and again it appears to suggest rather some thought of a transcendental body, wholly different from this body of flesh and blood. So especially in 2 Corinthians v. 1-9, with its wonderful vision, after the dissolution of 'our earthly house of this tabernacle', of 'a building of God, an house not made with hands, eternal in the heavens'.

On the theme, see especially the following articles:

H. Clavier, 'Brèves Remarques sur la notion de σῶμα πνευματικόν', in *The Background of the New Testament and its Eschatology: Studies in Honour of C. H. Dodd* (Cambridge: C.U.P., 1956), pp. 342-362.

O. Cullmann, *op. cit.* (see Additional Notes on i. 21 and iii. 11).

A. Feuillet, 'La Demeure céleste et la destinée des chrétiens: exégèse de II Cor. v. 1-10 et contribution à l'étude des fondements de l'eschatologie paulinienne', *RSR*, 44 (1956), pp. 161-192, 360-402.

W. Gutbrod, *Die paulinische Anthropologie*, III. B. 'Die Erneuerung des ganzen Menschen', pp. 224-245.

J. Héring, 'Eschatologie biblique et idéalisme platonicien', in *The Background of the N.T.*, pp. 444-463, especially pp. 460 ff.; and L. S. Thornton, *loc. cit.* (see notes on i. 21 f., *supra*).

On the positive side, the fundamental point to the Apostle is that the destiny of the Christian is to share the likeness of his Lord. Even now, he tells us, the transformation is proceeding within us. 'We all, with unveiled face mirroring the glory of the Lord, are being transformed into the same image from glory to glory, as by the Lord, the Spirit' (2 Cor. iii. 18). This transformation is to be made complete at his coming from heaven, when he **will refashion our body of lowliness to share the form of his body of glory.** He defines our destiny in similar terms in Romans viii. 29: 'For those whom [God] foreknew, he also foreordained to share the form of the image of his Son, to the end that he might be the firstborn among many brethren'.

The Apostle has not told us how he envisages the 'intermediate state' of the believer, between the time of his death and the Parousia of the Lord, when he is to be raised from the dead and given a body refashioned to share the form of Christ's body of glory. At times, he speaks of it as a 'sleep'; 'the dead in Christ' can be described also as 'those who have fallen asleep in Jesus' (1 Thess. iv. 14, 16); again, he is assured that 'to die is gain', and he has 'the desire to move on and to be with Christ, for that is far and away the better' (i. 23). He nowhere suggests that he thinks of it as a period of punishment for the expurgation of sins committed on earth (unless we find a hint of such a thought in 1 Cor. iii. 12-15). His one clear certainty is that 'God did not destine us unto wrath, but to the obtaining of salvation through our Lord Jesus Christ who died for us, that

whether we wake or sleep, we might live together with him'
(1 Thess. v. 9-10): so that 'if we live, we live unto the Lord;
and if we die, we die unto the Lord; therefore whether we live
or whether we die, we are the Lord's' (Rom. xiv. 8).

See also the Additional Notes: 'On Paul's Expectation of the
Life to Come'; and 'On the Hope of Resurrection' (following
the notes on i. 18-26, and on iii. 11, *above*).

His power . . . to bring all things into subjection to him- 21
self. The transformation which Christ is to effect in us at his
Parousia is not to be regarded as the natural destiny of man,
but as the accomplishment of Omnipotence. The phrase is
a reflection of the language of Psalm viii. 7, with which Paul
is accustomed to associate Psalm cx. 1; compare 1 Corinthians
xv. 22-28.

CHAPTER FOUR

I. (e) CONCLUSION AND POSTSCRIPT (continued)

13. PERSONAL APPEALS, AND FAREWELL GREET-INGS AND COUNSELS. iii. 1b; iv. 2-9.

(iii. 1b) To repeat the same pleas to you need not cause me trepidation, and for you it is safe. (iv. 2) I implore Evodia and I implore Syntyche to be united in the Lord. (3) Yes, and I ask you also, true comrade—help them; for they contended at my side in the cause of the gospel along with Clement, too, and with the rest of my fellow workers, whose names are in the book of life. (4) I bid you farewell in the Lord, always; again I shall say, Fare you well. (5) Let your kindliness be perceived by all men. The Lord is near. (6) Never be fretful, but by continual prayer and supplication, with thanksgiving, let your requests be made known to God; (7) and the peace of God, which surpasses all imagination, will guard your hearts and thoughts in Christ Jesus.

(8) Finally, brethren, let your minds dwell on whatever is true, whatever is worthy of reverence, whatever is upright, whatever is pure, whatever is lovely, whatever is esteemed—all that pertains to virtue, all that merits praise. (9) What you learned and received, and what you heard and saw in me, put this in practice; and the God of peace will be with you.

After the long interpolation, we come back to the closing paragraphs of the main letter. Paul has begun to write his closing greetings: 'Finally, my brethren, I bid you farewell in the Lord' (iii. 1a). But at the last moment, he feels that his pleas for unity have left something necessary unsaid. He knows that the root of the disharmony in the church of Philippi is the

rivalry of two outstanding women, **Evodia** and **Syntyche**; and
he now makes bold to address a special plea directly to them,
with all the added force of the last wish of a man facing death.

The same pleas—those of i. 27 and ii. 2-4; pleas for unity iii. 1b
of disposition, of soul and spirit; for humility; and for concern
for the rights of others. The literal rendering—'to write the
same things'—has led to the suggestion that the words are an
introduction to the matters expounded in the interpolated
passage, and that they refer to a lost letter in which Paul had
discussed the same theme. Erasmus thinks rather of oral
warnings which the Apostle had given.

Need not cause me trepidation—literally, 'to me is not
fearsome'. The adjective ὀκνηρός, which is interpreted as
meaning 'fearsome' or 'giving rise to trepidation', is used
elsewhere in the New Testament in the sense of 'indolent' or
'slothful' (Matt. xxv. 26; Rom. xii. 11). The usage here is
distinctly literary (cf. Sophocles, *Oedipus Rex*, 834; where the
Chorus gives expression to the apprehensions which it has felt
on hearing Oedipus tell how he killed Laius: 'To us also, O
King, this story is cause for trepidation'). The phrase 'to me
not fearsome, and for you safe' is in Greek a line of verse
(iambic trimeter), and it is probable that Paul is quoting, half
playfully, from a poem unknown to us.[1] He is actually plucking
up all his courage to address the women directly, to bid them
take to heart personally all that he has said to the whole church
about the need for unity among themselves. We are inclined to
feel that the 'partisanship' and the 'vain ambition' which he
deprecates (ii. 3) have a specific application to these two women,
each of them feeling that her services and her abilities are
outstanding and entitle her to a superior place; with the almost
inevitable result that the members of the congregation would
take sides in the dispute, some favouring the claims of Evodia
and some those of Syntyche. No one who has ever had the
duties of pastoral care of a parish will need to be told how much
dynamite is stored in such a situation. Here too we may see the
significance of the repeated 'all' of the earlier chapters. Paul
makes it clear that he makes no distinction in his affection and
in his prayers for them: he prays for them *all* (i. 3), he longs for

[1] See also Moule, *Idiom Book*, p. 199, n. 1.

them *all* (i. 8), he hopes to continue with them *all* (i. 25), he rejoices with them *all* (ii. 17); and he assures them that Epaphroditus is longing for them *all*.

iv. 2 The same desire to avoid the slightest appearance of favouritism is probably the cause of the repetition of the verb **implore;** the two women are addressed in exactly the same terms. It has often been suggested that either Evodia or Syntyche is to be identified with the Lydia of Acts 16, 'Lydia' being simply the feminine form of the adjective 'Lydian' (the woman was a native of Thyatira in Lydia). In view of the prominence of Lydia in the story of the founding of the church, one would indeed expect her name to be mentioned here. Some have tried to identify her with the **true comrade** of the following verse, but this is ruled out by the fact that the adjective is used in the masculine form.

3 **True comrade**—it would be hard to find a phrase which has been attacked with as much ingenuity as has been devoted to this one. Who, in the Philippian church, would recognize himself and be recognized by all the others, as the person addressed in these words? Partly as an exhibit of curiosities, we may list some of the suggestions that have been offered. (1) Luke, taken to be the author of the 'We-document' of Acts and of the book as a whole; this conjecture rests upon the observation that Acts begins to use the first person at the time of the decision to go into Macedonia (xvi. 10), ceases to use it before the story of the Philippian mission is concluded, and resumes it only at the time of the departure from Philippi on the way to Jerusalem for Paul's last visit (xx. 5). It is suggested that Luke had remained all the intervening years in Philippi, and that Paul now appeals to him as his **true comrade** to help the two women to resolve their dispute amicably. (2) Lydia (see note on verse 2, above); perhaps the wildest of all the conjectures is that Paul addresses Lydia as his wife! (σύζυγος—**comrade** —means literally 'yokefellow'). Apart from the grammatical impossibility of this interpretation, it is obvious that Paul was unmarried—how could a married man write 1 Corinthians vii, especially verses 7-9 and 32-34? Yet even Erasmus fell into this trap; he paraphrases: 'vera germanaque coniunx!' (3) Epaphroditus, the bearer of the letter; it is held by some that

Epaphroditus had been sent home to Philippi earlier. (4) Σύζυγος is taken by some as a personal name—Syzygus. This is by no means impossible, but no trace of such a name has been discovered anywhere else. We would think forthwith of the 'rector' or 'bishop' of Philippi, if there were the slightest grounds for supposing that the church had a leader occupying an analogous position. All we can say is that the words point to some man of tact and influence, who can intervene to help the two women resolve their differences; he might well need a word from the Apostle to overcome his reluctance to make the attempt. **Help them**—certainly in the sense of helping them to become loyal friends again—**united in the Lord.**

Contended at my side—he pays tribute to their courageous and energetic co-operation with him in the struggles of earlier days, when the church was ringed with foes. Again he borrows the language of the games; he depicts the struggle for the gospel as a contest in which they have been pitted along with him 'against principalities and powers . . . against the spiritual hosts of wickedness in the heavenly places' (Eph. vi. 12; cf. i. 27, *note*), who employ the human opponents of the gospel as their tools. **Clement** is otherwise unknown to us; the name is Roman (Clemens). **The book of life**—the roll of those whom God has 'appointed to obtain salvation' (1 Thess. v. 9). The notion of a **book** in which God has written the names of the faithful is found often in the Old Testament (Ex. xxxii. 32 f.; Ps. lxix. 28; etc.); it is a figure of predestination (see especially Ps. cxxxix. 16: 'In thy book were all my members written, which in continuance were fashioned, when as yet there was none of them'). In apocalyptic, **the book** becomes the record by which men are judged at the Last Judgment (Dan. xii. 1; cf. Apoc. xx. 12-15). And our Lord bids his disciples 'rejoice, not that the spirits are subject to you, but . . . because your names are written in heaven' (Luke x. 20). The phrase here seems to convey the thought that Paul is speaking of **Clement . . . and the rest of my fellow workers** as of comrades who have died in the faith.

Fare well, as in iii. 1a, is expressed by the imperative of 4 the verb 'rejoice', the usual Greek salutation given either at meeting or at parting. Here it may retain an undertone of the literal sense ('rejoice in the Lord always'—AV), but only to the extent that our own 'good-bye' retains a faint touch of the underlying 'God be with you'. Professor Goodspeed suggests the rendering: 'Good-bye, and the Lord be always with you' (*Problems of New Testament Translation*, 174 f.).

5 **Your kindliness**—Paul uses the cognate noun in 2 Corinthians x. 1, in speaking of 'the gentleness and kindliness of Christ'. These words of the ethical vocabulary have no exact equivalents in another language. They have an aesthetic element in them, and carry the content that they have acquired through usage in countless contexts. Paul suggests that the Christian community should be known for **kindliness,** courtesy, forbearance, considerate thoughtfulness; **all men** should recognize this quality of life among the believers, even though they hate them for it and rage against the gospel of grace which has created this spirit among them. **The Lord is near**—another indication of the vividness of expectation with which he looks for the coming of Jesus in glory. Christians are to live 'like men who are awaiting their Master' (Luke xii. 36); and their conduct and character are determined by that expectation and not by the hostility of the world in which they live. **Near** is certainly to be taken in this temporal sense; the Apostle is not speaking of the nearness of the Lord in his abiding presence with us, but of the imminence of his coming to establish his kingdom. One of the earliest prayers of the church was 'Marana tha!' ('Our Lord, come!'); and the great Apocalypse of John closes on this note: 'Come, Lord Jesus!' (Apoc. xxii. 20).

6 The following verses echo the teaching of the Sermon on the Mount. Trust in the fatherly care of God and in his providence is the remedy for all our anxieties (Matt. vi. 25-34). **Never be fretful**—from a human point of view, Paul himself had plenty of things to worry about, as a prisoner uncertain whether he would be set free or sentenced to death; and the people to whom he writes had ample cause for worry in the hostility of their neighbours and the constant threat of persecution. He is not speaking of imaginary troubles or unreal anxieties, but of serious threats and difficulties, of imminent and pressing dangers. If he bids them have no anxiety—**never be fretful**—

it is not because he makes light of the troubles which they face, but because he knows that God is greater than all our troubles. **By continual prayer and supplication with thanksgiving** (the rendering 'in everything, by prayer . . .' is also possible, but less satisfactory)—the teaching is far removed from the Stoic discipline of 'Apathy', the cultivation of an ability to remain unaffected by anything outside one's own control; the Stoic knew nothing of a God to whom he could make supplication. Paul bids his readers turn with the confidence of beloved children to the heavenly Father who 'will give good things to those who ask him' (Matt. vii. 11). **Thanksgiving** for the benefits received at his hands in the past will confirm our trust that he will not fail us in the present or in the future. **Prayer . . . with thanksgiving** will cause our fears and worries to melt away; for when we **let [our] requests be made known to God,** we look beyond the difficulties of our present situation to the unseen Power and Love with whom all things are possible. **The peace of God** is first of all the peace which God himself 7 possesses, and then the peace which God bestows upon all who lay their cares before him **by prayer and supplication with thanksgiving.** God is not himself beset with anxieties, for he knows the end from the beginning and directs all things in accordance with his will; he is never at the mercy of circumstances. We have nothing resembling the same kind of control over the conditions that affect our lives; and we cannot summon up for ourselves the same kind of peace in the presence of needs which we cannot supply or of threatening troubles which we are powerless to avert. But if we are content to trust God, and to leave our difficulties to his disposing, he imparts to us his peace. **Guard** is a word of the military vocabulary. Our **hearts** may quake for fear; our **thoughts** may run away with us and make cowards of us; but when we turn to God in prayer, we have the assurance of the Apostle that **the peace of God will guard [our] hearts and thoughts in Christ Jesus.** His peace will protect us against our own inward failings as well as against threats from without. **Surpasses all imagination**—this interpretation seems to be that of the Latin Vulgate (*exsuperat omnem sensum*), but it is possible also to take the phrase in the sense that God's peace is better than anything which we can devise for ourselves, better than anything that our minds can create for us. We cannot 'think' our worries away, but when we bring them before God in prayer, he gives us *his* peace, which is far better than any calmness which we could achieve by reasoning.

8   With another **finally, brethren** (as in iii. 1), Paul indicates again that he is approaching the end of his letter; it is scarcely possible to imagine that he writes this knowing that he has still to express his thanks for the gifts brought by Epaphroditus. This confirms our suggestion that verses 10 to 20 belong to an earlier letter (see Introduction, sec. I, 'Authenticity and Integrity of the Epistle', and the notes on the passage which follows). The striking feature about the injunction to **let your minds dwell on whatever is true, worthy of reverence, lovely,** etc., is that Paul here sanctifies, as it were, the generally accepted virtues of pagan morality. None of the words which he uses is specifically Christian; some of them are not found elsewhere in the New Testament, and several are not used in any other letter of Paul's. It is almost as if he had taken a current list from a textbook of ethical instruction, and made it his own; these are nothing else than the virtues of the copybook maxims. It follows that Paul had come to recognize that there was a genuine capacity for moral discernment in the pagan society around him, and that the things which were counted honourable by good men everywhere were in fact worthy of honour, worthy to be cultivated by a Christian believer. **Let your minds dwell on . . . all that pertains to virtue,** etc.—the verb λογίζεσθε signifies not merely 'meditate upon', or 'think on these things' (AV), but 'take them into account', 'give them weight in your decisions'. **Virtue** (ἀρετή), the most comprehensive Greek term for moral excellence and the central theme of Greek ethics, occurs only here in the writings of Paul. To the Stoics, it was the highest good, the only end to which a man should devote himself; the fact that it is used only once by Paul is enough of itself to show that he was not so much indebted to the Stoics as is sometimes claimed (see Bibliography, section ii 'Special Studies', (c). 'On Paul and Stoicism'). **Praise**—Paul as a rule thinks only of what God will praise; here he clearly speaks of the kind of conduct that wins the praise of men. He is

seldom concerned with human approval (see especially 1 Cor.
iv. 3-5); certainly he does not regard the moral standards of
society as having any ultimate validity.

III.—A LETTER OF THANKS

14. PAUL EXPRESSES HIS JOY IN THE GENEROSITY OF THE PHILIPPIANS. iv. 10-20

(10) It was a great joy to me in the Lord that now at length
you gave effect to your concern for me—in that you were
continually concerned, but were unable to find occasion.
(11) Not that I speak as if complaining of want; for I have
learned how to be sufficient to myself in the conditions
in which I am. (12) I have been schooled to indigence;
I have been schooled also to abundance. In everything
and in all circumstances I have become adept, whether
to be full fed or to go hungry, whether to be amply
supplied or to be in want. (13) I have strength for all, in
him who makes me strong. (14) Nevertheless, you did
what was right in making yourselves my partners in this
affliction; (15) and you know yourselves, Philippians, that
in the beginning of the gospel, when I went out from
Macedonia, no church but you alone entered into partnership with me in an accounting of receipts and expenditures; (16) for even in Thessalonica you sent me supplies
to meet my needs, more than once. (17) It is not the gift
that I seek; what I seek is the interest that goes on multiplying to your account. (18) I have received payment in
full, and have enough and to spare; I am fully supplied,
now that I have received from Epaphroditus the things
that he brought from you—' a pleasing odour,' a sacrifice
acceptable, well-pleasing to God. (19) And my God shall
fully supply every need of yours gloriously, in accordance
with his wealth, in Christ Jesus. (20) To our God and
Father be glory unto the ages of ages. Amen.

These verses can hardly be regarded as a part of the letter which Epaphroditus is to carry with him on his return to Philippi. It is written around Paul's formal acknowledgment of the gifts from the Philippian church which Epaphroditus had delivered on his arrival, some months earlier (even on the hypothesis of an Ephesian origin, it would be several weeks earlier.) In the meantime, Epaphroditus has fallen seriously ill and has recovered enough to be able again to travel (ii. 26-28), and word of his illness and of the Philippians' distress over it has gone to and fro. It is inconceivable that Paul should wait all that time to express his thanks for the gifts which the Christians of Philippi had sent him. E. F. Scott has tried to overcome this objection by suggesting that Paul had of course sent a letter of thanks for the supplies as soon as he received them, and that this is a second tribute to the Philippians for their generosity. Such a suggestion is quite untenable; apart from the fact. that we have before us a singularly delicate expression of appreciation, which would lose much of its appeal if it were to be regarded as a second, much belated and (under such circumstances) studied and rather fulsome essay, it must be observed that he uses the technical word ἀπέχω—**I have received**—found on thousands of commercial documents to acknowledge the receipt of money or goods; a word as unmistakable as the mark of a rubber stamp on a bill, PAID. This alone would be enough to tell us that we are reading Paul's receipt for the gifts from Philippi. We cannot doubt that this is the very letter sent by Paul as soon as the gifts were brought to him. It is possible, of course, that this is only a fragment of his letter; but it is quite possible that only the salutation is missing, or even that it was identical with the salutation of the later letter (i. 1-2). The closing sentences (iv. 21-23) of greetings and benediction, which we are taking as the end of the letter, may almost as readily be taken as the conclusion of this letter of thanks; only the greetings from 'all the saints, especially those of Caesar's household' would come more naturally after a stay of some months than on the morrow of Paul's arrival.

10   If we may attempt to picture the state of Paul's mind at the time of his arrival in Rome, we shall have a vivid sense of the **great joy in the Lord** which he felt when Epaphroditus met

him laden with gifts from his old friends at Philippi. He came
to Rome, we shall remember, as a prisoner in the custody of
armed guards, at the end of a terrible voyage in which his ship
had been driven from her course by gales and finally wrecked
on the coast of Malta. He had been a prisoner for nearly three
years, and he was coming into a strange city, where he had no
personal friends and could not be sure of the kind of reception
that awaited him among the Christians. On that point, he was
quickly reassured, for word of his arrival at Puteoli was sent ahead
to Rome and some of 'the brethren' went down to meet him
at Appii Forum and some at Three Taverns, along the Appian
Way (Acts xxviii. 15); but even after this welcome, it is not hard
to imagine his delight at the coming of Epaphroditus and at
the assurance that his friends of Philippi were thinking of him
and eager to help him once again, as they had so often done
before.

Now at length—without the slightest insinuation that there
has been any undue delay; it is to remove any possible thought
of reproach in his words that he adds **you were continually
concerned, but were unable to find occasion. Gave
effect to your concern**—literally, 'caused your concern for
me to put forth fresh shoots'; it is the figure of a bush or tree
making new growth in the spring. This verb ($\dot{a}\nu\epsilon\theta\dot{a}\lambda\epsilon\tau\epsilon$) and
also $\dot{\eta}\kappa\alpha\iota\rho\epsilon\hat{\iota}\sigma\theta\epsilon$ **(you were unable to find occasion,** 'you
were without opportunity') are found nowhere else in the New
Testament and are rare elsewhere. This little letter contains an
exceptionally large proportion of *hapax legomena*—no less than
five words. The lack of opportunity could lie either in the
Apostle's circumstances or in pressing difficulties at Philippi;
either he had not needed their help or they had not been in a
position to give him any.

Paul is not going to pull a poor mouth in the hope of enticing 11
more gifts from them; indeed, he seems reluctant to admit that
he has experienced any shortage of supplies at all. He was
always embarrassed by having to depend upon other people for
his support; and made a point, as far as possible, of earning
what he needed for subsistence by working with his own hands,
even though he knew that 'the Lord commanded those who
proclaim the gospel to live of the gospel', just as those who

minister in the temple live of the offerings (1 Cor. ix. 13-14). He can even recognize that the spiritual blessings which he brings are far greater than any material return that his hearers may make (1 Cor. ix. 11: 'If we sowed the things of the spirit for you, is it a great matter if we reap your things of the flesh?' cf. Rom. xv. 27); and he enjoins his churches to provide for the sustenance of their teachers (Gal. vi. 6). Yet he hates to accept such provision for his own needs. There may be an element of false pride here, yet we cannot but respect this fierce urge to be independent. Professor Dodd remarks acutely: 'He can scarcely bring himself to acknowledge that the money was welcome to him. . . . This was a man who had chosen poverty as his lot for ideal ends, but could never feel himself one of the "poor", to whom alms might be offered without suspicion of offence. He was indeed no aristocrat, but he had the feelings of a well-to-do *bourgeois*' (*New Testament Studies* [Manchester: M.U.P., 1953], 4. 'The Mind of Paul: I', pp. 72 f.). He always had the feeling that he was demeaning himself by accepting support; he was far happier when he could say: 'I will not be burdensome to you: for I seek not your's, but you; for the children ought not to lay up for the parents, but the parents for the children' (2 Cor. xii. 14; cf. Acts xx. 33-35). So he will not **speak as if complaining of want;** yet we may read between the lines that he was in fact in dire need, for he goes on to explain that he has learned how to manage on very little, to 'make do', as we say, with inadequate resources.

11   **Sufficient to myself**—Paul here uses a characteristic term of the Stoic (and Cynic) philosophers. An important part of their self-discipline was to reduce their needs to a minimum; the famous Cynic Diogenes, when he noticed a child drinking out of its hands, threw away his cup, saying, 'A child has vanquished me in economy' (Diogenes Laertius, *Lives and Opinions of Eminent Philosophers*, VI. 37). The 'self-sufficient' man was he who had rendered himself independent of external circumstances. Paul claims this ideal for himself; he evidently felt a certain admiration for the capacity of these wandering prophets of Virtue to endure hardness. Yet he is not devoted to hardship for its own sake. Unlike the Cynic, he does not go out 12 of his way to get along on as little as possible. **I have been**

schooled to indigence: I have been schooled also to abundance. He does not value the one above the other.

I have become adept—again he uses a technical term, borrowed this time from the mystery cults; it means literally, 'I have been initiated'; as if the vicissitudes of his life were the rites of admission to a secret society.

The 'self-sufficiency' of the Apostle is not after all the same 13 as the *autarkeia* of the Stoic, even though he has used the Stoic word a moment before. The Stoic knew no Power outside himself from whom he might derive strength to bear the hardships of life and to move untroubled through its changing circumstances. Paul has **strength for all,** but it is not his own acquired power of endurance; it is the strength that flows into him from his communion with Christ. **I have strength for all, in him who makes me strong.** He does not think of himself as a strong soul, who needs no outside support. He has schooled himself to be independent of outward circumstances, but he has no thought of denying his need of Christ and his reliance upon the strength which Christ supplies. Let us compare with this the remarkable passage in which he speaks of his weaknesses, which make him all the more receptive instrument of Christ's strength, which 'is made perfect in weakness'; and goes on, 'Most gladly, then, will I rather glory in my weaknesses, that the power of Christ may rest upon me. Therefore I am content with weaknesses . . . and hardships, for the sake of Christ; for when I am weak, then am I strong' (2 Cor. xii. 9-10).

You did what was right—the words reflect a phrase that is 14 commonly used (in the future tense) in letters of instruction or invitation; as, 'You will do what is right in accompanying Ailurion, the bearer of this note, to buy young pigeons for us for the feast' (from a Berlin papyrus letter of the first century; it is usually followed by the aorist participle, as here [*see* Moulton and Milligan, *Vocabulary*, s.v. ποιέω]). In such cases, it is about equivalent to our 'Be good enough to' (fulfil such and such a task). Here it is transferred into an acknowledgment that the task has been fulfilled. Paul is trying, still rather curtly, to overcome any touch of ungraciousness in his assurance that he could have got along quite well without the gifts which they had been good enough to send.

15   He now recalls gratefully the aid which he had received from
them in earlier times. The thought requires no elucidation, but
there are a number of unusual forms and expressions which call
for comment. **Philippians**—Paul uses a form which appears
to occur nowhere else except in the address of Polycarp's
epistle to the same church, where it is probably imitated from
this passage. The regular Greek forms are Φιλιππεῖς and
Φιλιππηνοί; the form in our text—Φιλιππήσιοι—is a Graecizing
of the Latin word *Philippenses*, and is an illustration of the
effects of the mixed culture of the colony; or perhaps even more
of Paul's fondness for adaptations of Latin forms (see W. M.
Ramsay, 'On the Greek Form of the Name Philippians,' in
JTS, i [1900], p. 116). Collart suggests that Paul's use of the
Latinized form here is 'a delicate compliment to the Latin
character of the city' (*Philippes*, p. 212 f.). **In the beginning of
the gospel**—in what sense could Paul so think of the relatively
recent time when he **went out from Macedonia?** Before that,
he had himself been preaching the faith for at least fourteen
years (perhaps for as much as seventeen) in 'the regions of
Syria and Cilicia' (Gal. i. 18-ii. 1); he had gone with Barnabas
through Cyprus and southern Galatia (Acts xiii-xiv); and others
had been active in the work of the gospel for some years before
his conversion. The phrase is doubly difficult if it be supposed
that this letter was written from an imprisonment in Ephesus,
less than five years after his departure from Macedonia. Is he
for the moment thinking of Christian history from the reader's
point of view—that it was soon after **the beginning of the
gospel** *in their province*? Or is he so much under the spell of
Greek civilization that he thinks of the victorious march of the
gospel as getting seriously under way only when the Greek
peninsula itself was invaded? Or may we suppose that he has
come to think of his arrival in Rome as a symbolic occupation
of the world's capital city by the vanguard of the Christian
forces, and is thus able to think of his first approach to a Roman
colony and his march along the Egnatian Way as the opening
of the decisive campaign? Such an interpretation would be more
appealing if he spoke of when he came into Macedonia, instead
of when he went out. It is hard to feel satisfied with any of the
explanations offered. **Partnership . . . accounting of receipts**

and expenditures—he heaps up business terms; in the following verses he will introduce still more of them—**the interest that goes on multiplying to your account; I have received** 17-18 **payment; I am fully supplied.** Professor Dodd is probably right in his suggestion that Paul 'covers up his embarrassment by piling up technical terms of trade, as if to give the transaction a severely "business" aspect' (*op. cit.*, p. 72). It may be that he has in the back of his mind some thought of striking a balance, with the spiritual benefits of the gospel entered to his credit and the material gifts of the Philippians credited to them; or (more likely), he is anticipating the assurance that God, out of his matchless wealth, will repay the advances made to Paul by his Philippian friends. **My God shall fully supply every** 19 **need of yours, gloriously, in accordance with his wealth, in Christ Jesus.** The gifts of the Philippians are a loan which will be repaid by God, and all the while it will be drawing compound interest. It scarcely needs to be said that he does not think of **the interest which goes on multiplying** in terms of an improvement in their material wellbeing; but that the gift enriches the giver in the far more precious things of the spirit. καρπόν—**interest;** literally 'fruit', is often used of the 'profit' to be gained in a business transaction. Here the present participle πλεονάζοντα, 'continuing to multiply', suggests that he is using the figure of compound interest. All through, he appears to be attempting a touch of the whimsical, to avoid labouring the expression of his thanks; but beneath it is the profound conviction that the exercise of generosity enlarges the spirit and opens it to receive a divine blessing that must far exceed the gift, in accordance with the wealth of the divine giver. For the whole thought, compare Luke vi. 37: 'Give, and it will be given to you; good measure, pressed down, shaken together, running over, will they put into your bosom'; and the eloquent plea of 2 Corinthians ix.

Even in Thessalonica you sent me supplies . . . more 16 **than once.** The words have a bearing upon the length of the mission in Thessalonica, which must have continued for more than the three weeks mentioned in Acts xvii. 2. In writing to the Thessalonians, Paul does not mention that the Philippian church had contributed to his support, but reminds them that

he and his companions were 'working night and day, that we
might not put a burden upon you' (1 Thess. ii. 9). It follows
that the gifts of the Philippians were sufficient to cover only a
part of his expenses. It is interesting to see how quickly the
missionary spirit burgeoned in Paul's converts. Only a few
weeks after they have received the gospel themselves, and while
they are still suffering from the enforced departure of the
founders of their little Christian cell, they are eager to have
a share in the evangelization of Thessalonica and to accept a
measure of responsibility for the furtherance of the mission.
Similarly, the Thessalonians in their turn were quick to engage
in the missionary enterprise (1 Thess. i. 8).

18   **I have received**—ἀπέχω; the term most frequently used in
acknowledging payments, especially in documents of the first
century A.D. (U. Wilcken, *Griechische Ostraka*, Bk. I [Leipzig:
Von Giesecke & Devrient, 1899], chap iii, pp. 80-87).

In the second part of this verse, Paul drops his commercial
language to adopt the language of sacrifice. **A pleasing odour**—
a phrase quoted from Lxx, which was originally used of the
burnt offering, and has in it traces of the primitive anthropo-
morphism which thought of God as enjoying the smell of the
roasting flesh, and allowing his wrath to be appeased (so in
Gen. viii. 21: 'Yahweh smelled the pleasing odour; and Yahweh
said in his heart, I will not again curse the earth'). In later
usage, it appears to become a synonym for sacrifice of any kind,
as in Ezekiel xvi. 19, where it applies to offerings of cereals, and
oil, and honey, which were not burned. Paul turns it into a pure
metaphor, though still in a context of **sacrifice**; the gifts of the
Philippians are compared to an offering laid upon the altar of
God.

19   **Every need of yours**—not alone material, but spiritual.
God's supply will be abundant in proportion to his limitless
wealth. **Gloriously**—literally 'in glory' (ἐν δόξῃ); the phrase
can hardly be given a local or temporal sense, as if it meant 'in
the realm of the heavenly', or 'in the beatitude of the life to
come' ('by placing you in glory'—Lightfoot). In the context,
it is the supplying of their needs in the circumstances of the
present life that he has in mind. **In Christ Jesus**—as always,
Paul sees the action of God towards man as taking place in the

sphere of the common life which flows from Christ and is shared with him. God acts **in Christ Jesus,** and makes his grace and power known among those who are **in Christ Jesus.**

The little letter of thanks closes with an ascription of **glory** 20 to God as **our Father,** who provides for the needs of all his children. In its original form, of course, this may have been followed by a few lines of greeting and a benediction.

Despite the touch of embarassment, the element of constraint which makes itself manifest, the Apostle has given us in these few lines one of the gems of literature. Though he has never actually expressed a word of thanks, he has given moving testimony of his profound appreciation of the gift and of the loving spirit which prompted it. And there are few paragraphs to be found in his epistles which reflect more clearly the essential nobility of his character and the delicacy of his mind, together with his capacity both to give and to win affection.

I. (e) CONCLUSION AND POSTSCRIPT (completed)

15. CLOSING GREETINGS AND BENEDICTION.
iv. 21-23

(21) Greet every saint in Christ Jesus. The brethren who are with me send you their greetings. (22) All the saints send you their greetings, especially those of Caesar's household. (24) The grace of the Lord Jesus Christ be with your spirit.

Paul sends his own greetings, and adds the greetings of his associates and of the local church. **Every saint**—Paul wants his good wishes expressed to each individual member of the Philippian church. But who is to convey the greetings? Who may we take to be the subject of the imperative **greet**? A trifle such as this makes us realize how little we know about organization and procedure in these early churches. Clearly his words imply that there are some responsible leaders who will convey his greetings to the others. **In Christ Jesus** may be construed either with the verb or with the noun, or (perhaps better) with both. It is the relationship with Christ, the incorporation into his body, that makes a man a **saint;** his life is transferred into the realm of the holy, of that which belongs to God, by virtue of his being **in Christ Jesus.** At the same time, the Apostle extends his greeting **in Christ Jesus,** just as he 'hopes in the Lord' to send Timothy (ii. 19), and bids them 'fare well in the Lord' (iii. 1, iv. 4); for all his relations with them are grounded in their common association with Christ. **The brethren who are with me** will of course include Timothy, and perhaps others of Paul's associates who had come to Rome to join him 22 and to continue working under his direction. **All the saints** will then be taken to mean the members of the Roman church itself. **Caesar's household**—not members of the imperial family, but persons employed in the domestic and administrative establishment of the Emperor. Most of them would be slaves and freedmen; and a large proportion of them would be from the eastern provinces—Greeks, Anatolians, Syrians, and Egyptians. It is known that Nero's mistress Poppaea was a Jewess, or more precisely a proselyte to Judaism; and it is unlikely that if there had been conversions to Christianity within the highest circles at this time, there would be no trace of them in our sources. The imperial civil service was of course immense, and would have its bureaux in all the towns and cities of the Empire; so that the phrase in itself is no indication that the writer is in Rome. It is perhaps not superfluous to add that it does not tell against a Roman origin; the **household** must have numbered hundreds, if not thousands of employees in the capital. If **the saints ... of Caesar's household** are mentioned as **especially** desiring to send greetings to Philippi, it would seem to follow that some of them must have been Macedonians or Thracians—perhaps even natives of Philippi itself.

23   The benediction is unique, in the substitution of the phrase **with your spirit** for the more usual 'with you'. The singular **spirit** perhaps reflects the thought that they are all animated by the one spirit.

THE 'KENOTIC' CHRISTOLOGY

By Eugene R. Fairweather

FOR the contemporary student of Christian theology, the centre of interest in the Epistle to the Philippians is almost certain to be the great soteriological hymn in Phil. ii. 5-11, and more particularly the two words ἑαυτὸν ἐκένωσεν (he stripped himself, or emptied himself). This phrase has given both a name and a strong impetus to a movement of Christological thought which has been described by a judicious critic as 'the fourth great attempt at theological explanation of the being of Christ', worthy of mention along with the Pauline and Johannine Christologies, the conciliar definitions, and the scholastic interpretations of the hypostatic union (P. Henry, S.J., art. 'Kénose', *Dict. de la Bible*, Supplément, v. 156). Of course, as both its defenders and its critics acknowledge, the 'Kenotic' Christology does not depend on Phil. ii. 7 alone. On the contrary, its immediate occasion was the development of historical study of the gospels and the concurrent emphasis on the authentic humanity of Jesus, while its background is to be found in certain tendencies of Protestant theological speculation and post-Cartesian philosophy. Nonetheless, we may still wonder whether the theory would have taken its distinctive form or acquired its wide influence apart from its putative basis in Pauline teaching. The passage in Philippians is, after all, the only New Testament text that can plausibly be construed as a theological interpretation of the conditions under which the eternal Word entered into human life and death, and it alone speaks of the *kenosis* of him who, **being in the form of God,** took **the form of a slave** and **humbled himself.** It is true, as Professor Beare has shown in his exegesis, that any attempt to read back the problems and the solutions of developed Christological reflection into a primitive Christian hymn of this kind is exceedingly rash. While the hymn obviously has profound Christological implications, it is not itself an essay in Christology, and St. Paul does not reproduce it with any such purpose in mind. It has been effectively used, nevertheless, as part of the foundation for a supposedly 'biblical' Christology, deliberately set up over against the 'metaphysical' Christology of the Ecumenical Councils and the medieval schools. For this reason, it may be worthwhile to examine the relation of the Kenotic Christology to the Pauline text—and further, once we have seen how tenuous that relation is, to comment on the 'metaphysical' notions which form the real doctrinal basis of the Kenotic theory.

By a Kenotic Christology we mean a doctrine of the Incarnation which asserts some real modification of the divine attributes as a necessary condition of the true and personal entrance of the Son of God into human history and human experience. In a broader sense, of course, all Christology must be 'kenotic' if it is to be true to the central Christian tradition from the New Testament onwards. The Christian mind must not seek to evade the mystery of the redemptive action of the Lord of glory through the weakness and lowliness of the flesh.

> That the great Angel-blinding light should shrink
> His blaze, to shine in a poor Shepherd's eye.
> That the unmeasur'd God so low should sink,
> As Pris'ner in a few poor Rags to lie.
> That from his Mother's Breast he milk should drink,
> Who feeds with Nectar Heav'n's fair family.
>> That a vile Manger his low Bed should prove,
>> Who in a Throne of stars Thunders above.
>
> That he whom the Sun serves, should faintly peep
> Through clouds of Infant flesh: that he the old
> Eternal Word should be a Child, and weep.
> That he who made the fire, should fear the cold;
> That Heav'n's high Majesty his Court should keep
> In a clay-cottage, by each blast controll'd.
>> That Glory's self should serve our Griefs, and fears:
>> And free Eternity, submit to years.

These 'knotty Riddles' which Richard Crashaw so magnificently expresses (*Steps to the Temple*, 'Sospetto d' Herode') are the very stuff of Christology, and with the Kenoticists we must face the ineluctable witness of the Gospel to the generous humility of the everlasting Son who was made man. The point at issue in the Kenotic controversy, however, is whether this gracious action of God involved a depotentiation of deity. Kenotic Christology may speak, with Gottfried Thomasius, of a surrender of the 'relative attributes' of omnipotence, omniscience and omnipresence, or, with Wolfgang Friedrich Gess, of what amounts to an abdication of the Logos from the Godhead. (For a careful exposition of these and other Continental theories of *kenosis*, cf. A. B. Bruce, *The Humiliation of Christ* [2nd ed., Edinburgh: T. & T. Clark, 1881], Lect. IV.) In its more moderate forms, it may suggest a reduction of the divine attributes from actuality to potentiality—the view shared by Peter Taylor Forsyth and Hugh Ross Mackintosh—or perhaps postulate 'a ceasing to exercise, at least in a certain sphere, and *so far as human thought can attain*, some natural prerogatives of the divine existence' (to quote the almost unintelligibly cautious words of Charles Gore, *Dissertations on Subjects Connected with the Incarnation* [London: John Murray, 1895], p. 90). Despite their wide variety, however, all versions of the Kenotic theory rest on the principle succinctly stated by Mackintosh: 'No human life of God is possible without a prior self-adjustment of deity' (*The Doctrine of the Person of Jesus Christ* [3rd ed., Edinburgh: T. & T. Clark, 1914], p. 470). Consequently, a critical examination of this statement will amount to a test of Kenoticism as such; if it can be sustained, then we may go on to select our version of the theory, but if it proves indefensible, then no Kenotic speculation can be defended.

It can at least be said, to begin with, that the text itself gives us no reason to suppose that Kenotic ideas had ever entered St. Paul's head. 'Such an idea is as foreign to Paul as are the problems it is supposed to solve' (W. Morgan, *The Religion and Theology of Paul* [Edinburgh: T. & T. Clark, 1917], p. 66). To Professor Beare's exegesis, which coincides with this judgment, we may add the still useful remarks of M. R. Vincent:

> As regards ἑαυτὸν ἐκένωσεν, any attempt to commit Paul to a precise theological statement of the limitations of Christ's humanity involves the reader in a hopeless maze. The word

ἐκένωσεν was evidently selected as a peculiarly strong expression of the entireness of Jesus' self-renunciation, and in order to throw the pre-incarnate glory and the incarnate humiliation into sharp contrast; to show that Christ utterly renounced and laid aside the majesty which he possessed in his original state. Its most satisfactory definition is found in the succeeding details which describe the incidents of Christ's humanity, and with these exegesis is compelled to stop. The word does not indicate a surrender of deity, nor a paralysis of deity, nor a change of personality, nor a break in the continuity of self-consciousness (*Commentary*, p. 89).

We might profitably quote Karl Barth's full theological commentary on the passage, which follows the line indicated by Vincent (*Church Dogmatics*, IV/1 [Edinburgh: T. & T. Clark, 1956], p. 180), but there is really no need to labour the point. It is clear enough as it is that the supposed *locus classicus* for Kenoticism, literally interpreted, has in fact no direct bearing on the question.

If modern scholarly exegesis of Phil. ii. 7 regards Kenotic speculation as irrelevant, the older exegetical tradition of Christendom, from the early Fathers through the Middle Ages and beyond, goes still further and repudiates the principle of all such speculation in advance. In his compact treatment of the evidence, F. Loofs shows plainly that the idea of a reduction of the divine attributes in the Incarnation is altogether foreign to the mind of the Fathers (art. 'Kenosis', *E.R.E.*, vii. 680-687). His conclusion is clearly stated in his summary of the views of Irenaeus, Origen and Novatian:

> Here the Kenosis is that self-limitation of the Logos which was involved in His manifestation in a human form, though at the same time He is not in any way limited as to His cosmic position. This conception of the Kenosis may be regarded as the recognized view of the early Church (*art. cit.* p. 684).

Loofs' view is reinforced by P. Henry's recent and more extensive account of patristic exegesis (*art. cit.* cols. 56-136). On the strength of these and other standard surveys it is safe to say that at best Christian antiquity considered notions of the 'self-adjustment of deity' only to reject them. It is striking enough that the Fathers, constantly preoccupied though they were with the fundamental issues of Christology, do not seem even to have suspected that a Kenotic interpretation of Phil. ii. 7 (or, for that matter, of any other New Testament text) would help them with their problems. As Henry says, 'the very silence of tradition is eloquent' (*art. cit.* col. 133). But the way in which tradition dealt with the idea of divine mutability—the underlying assumption of the Kenotic theories—was more eloquent still.

In view of the solidity and consistency of the traditional exegesis, a few examples, covering something like ten centuries and representing both Eastern and Western commentators, may prove instructive. (Unless otherwise indicated, quotations are taken from commentaries on Philippians ii. 6 ff.). We begin with an uncompromising statement by Origen:

> As to his having descended among men, he was originally 'in the form of God', and through love towards mankind 'emptied himself', that men might be capable of receiving him. . . . But if the immortal God, the Word, seems to Celsus to undergo a change and transformation by taking a mortal body and a human soul, let him learn that the Word, still remaining in essence the Word, suffers none of those things which the body or the soul suffers (*C. Celsum*, iv. 15 [*G.C.S.*, 2. 284 f.]).

Since, however, this might be discounted as 'Origenistic', let us listen next to Origen's eminent critic, Methodius of Olympus:

> Having 'emptied himself' and taken upon him the 'form of a slave', he was restored again to his former perfection and dignity. For he, being humbled and apparently degraded, was restored from his humiliation and degradation to his former completeness and greatness, having never been diminished from his essential perfection (*Symposium*, viii. 11 [*G.C.S.*, 27. 95 f.]).

Or let us look at Antiochene exegesis, as represented by a fragment of Theodore of Mopsuestia: '"Taking the form of a slave", he hid that dignity, being thought by those who saw him to be just what he appeared' (*In Epistolas B. Pauli Commentarii* [ed. H. B. Swete, Cambridge: University Press, 1880], i. 217). And then, as our last spokesman for the East, let us consult the distinguished Byzantine exegete, Theophylact:

> For him who is equal and of like power to God to be willing to become man, this is humility. . . . He chose to be humbled,

in such a way that in his humiliation he kept his high place. . . . For God the Word did not change into man, but he appeared as man, and, being formless [*aschematistos*], he came under an outward form [*schema*] (*P.G.*, 124. 1161 ff.).

Turning now to the West, we may begin with an often quoted dictum of Augustine: 'Thus he "emptied himself, taking the form of a servant", not losing the "form of God". The form of a servant was added; the form of God did not pass away' (*Sermo* 183. 4 [*P.L.*, 38. 990]). The principle thus straightforwardly stated, in terms whose theological clarity may be some compensation for what would seem to be a misunderstanding of the original sense of the word 'form' (*forma* = μορφή), was determinative for medieval exegesis. Sedulius Scotus puts it simply: 'He "emptied himself", not making void his substance, but yielding his honour' (*P.L.*, 103. 214). Rabanus Maurus expands the idea: 'He "emptied himself", not changing his own form, but "taking the form of a servant": nor was he altered or transformed into a man by the loss of his changeless immovability' (*P.L.*, 112. 489). Haymo of Auxerre offers a clear definition of the *kenosis*:

> He 'emptied himself', that is, he humbled himself and as it were diminished himself and made himself smaller. It is an emptying when a great and incomprehensible thing is comprehended in a small form. . . . The Word of God the Father, who is everywhere by the invisibility of his divinity, when he deigned to appear visibly in the small form of man, as it were emptied and humbled himself and (so to speak) in a way diminished himself. For he is above all things, outside all things, beneath all things, and whatsoever is, is within him (*P.L.*, 117. 740; on the authorship of this commentary, cf. C. Spicq, O.P., *Esquisse d'une histoire de l'exégèse latine au moyen-âge* [Paris: Vrin, 1944], pp. 50 f.).

As he goes on to make clear, this *kenosis* involves no change in the divine nature of the Word. Hervaeus of Bourg-Dieu stresses this principle when, after quoting our Augustinian text, he adds: 'He did not lose or diminish what he was, but he took what he was not. And in this way he both became less and remained equal' (*P.L.*, 181. 1292). All this Western exegesis is summed up, with typical clarity, by Thomas Aquinas:

Because he was full of divinity, did he therefore empty himself of divinity? No, because what he was he remained, and what he was not he took. . . . For as he came down from heaven, not because he ceased to be in heaven, but because he began to be in a new manner on earth, so also he emptied himself, not by laying down the divine nature, but by taking up human nature (*Super Epistolas S. Pauli Lectura*, Ad Phil., cap. 2, lect. 2 [Turin: Marietti, 1953, ii. 101]).

There is something impressive about the way in which this great chain of tradition excludes, on theological grounds, an interpretation of St. Paul which modern scholars dismiss on exegetical grounds. And yet one might argue that all this patristic and medieval exegesis is too explicitly theological—that equally with Kenotic exegesis it tries to answer questions which the Apostle had never thought of asking, and does so all too frequently at the expense of an accurate understanding of his terminology. There is a real difference, however, between the traditional position and Kenoticism. The traditional interpretation is not an attempt to foist on the text a theory of alien parentage; on the contrary, the sole concern of its exponents is to keep any conclusions drawn from St. Paul's statement under the control of the analogy of faith. It is in this contrast between the speculative exuberance of Kenoticism and the exegetical sobriety of the traditional view that the latter's strength is most conspicuous.

It should be obvious enough by now that the Kenotic Christology can make no serious claim for consideration as a 'biblical' interpretation of the Incarnation. Its defenders will still argue, however, that the New Testament presentation of the life of Christ cannot be satisfactorily interpreted on any other lines. On the one hand, we shall be reminded that the New Testament witness to Christ explicitly presents him as limited in knowledge, moved by human emotion, and subject to moral testing. 'The historical study of the Gospels has compelled a general recognition that the historical Jesus of Nazareth was humanly conditioned in His knowledge and in His entire consciousness' (J. M. Creed, in *Mysterium Christi* [ed. G. K. A. Bell and A. Deissmann, London: Longmans, 1930], pp. 132 f.). On the other hand, it will be pointed out that the New Testament theologians see in this full acceptance of the conditions of human existence the supreme manifestation of the limitless love of God for his unworthy creatures. When St. Paul writes that 'God commendeth his love toward us, in that, while we were yet sinners, Christ died for us' (Rom. v. 8), he is just putting in summary form a truth whose broad implications he and other New Testament writers spell out at length, as inherent in their Gospel. It is the keen awareness at once of the human facts and of their divine meaning that has led so many theologians —sometimes, at least, not without trepidation—to adopt some form of Kenoticism. Mackintosh expresses their concern very well:

> Somehow—to describe the method exactly may of course be beyond us—somehow God in Christ has brought His greatness down to the narrow measures of our life, becoming poor for our sake. This must be taken as seriously in dogmatic as in Christian piety, and a place must be found for the real fact which it denotes in our construction of the Incarnate life. . . . The difficulties of a Kenotic view are no doubt extremely grave; yet they are such as no bold construction can avoid, and in these circumstances it is natural to prefer a view which both conserves the vital religious interest in the self-abnegating descent of God (*Deus humilis*) and adheres steadfastly to the concrete details of the historical record (*op. cit.* p. 466).

Both of these motives—respect for the integrity of historical scholarship and desire to bear due witness to God's redemptive love—command our sympathy. We must ask, nevertheless, whether it is true that only a Kenotic doctrine can do them justice, and we must at least consider the possibility that only the introduction of certain presuppositions, extraneous both to the Kenoticists' fundamental motives and to the teaching of the New Testament, makes a Kenotic view seem inescapable. There are, in fact, two presuppositions whose influence can be clearly traced in the development of Kenotic speculation. The first of these is the peculiar variety of 'monophysitism' characteristic of Lutheran Christology, while the second is the tendency, typical of much modern philosophy, to define personality in terms of the natural activity of consciousness. The convergence of these two trends results in a disposition to construe unity of *person* as a functional unity of *nature* (or principle of action), and so to telescope the divine and human natures of the incarnate Word into one. When this disposition is linked to the Kenoticists' dual concern for the full recognition of Christ's humanity, the predictable outcome is an emphasis on the *human* functioning of Christ as defining his incarnate personality and, as an inevitable consequence, a virtual suppression of the divine nature. Mackintosh states the problem bluntly enough when he writes that Christ's 'life on earth was unequivocally human', so that 'the life Divine in Him found expression through human faculty, with a self-consciousness and activity mediated by His human *milieu*', and then goes on to say: 'We cannot predicate of Him two consciousnesses or two wills; the New Testament indicates nothing of the kind, nor indeed is it congruous with an intelligible psychology. The unity of His personal life is axiomatic' (*op. cit.* p. 469 f.). The phrase 'an intelligible psychology' gives the show away. What Mackintosh and those for whom he speaks expect of a Christology is an account of the reduction of deity and humanity to 'personal' unity, understood as the functional unity of a temporal, human consciousness. But this is a very large begging of the question—a fact that the Kenotic theologians would surely recognize if they were not held captive by their inherited presuppositions. With this in mind, it may be helpful to spell out these assumptions more explicitly.

The Lutheran 'monophysitism' to which we have referred is based on Luther's peculiar notion of the *communicatio idiomatum*.

> The catholic doctrine . . . teaches an ascription of the divine and the human properties to the Person who possesses the natures to which they pertain. There is no intercommunication of natural properties between the two natures, but their concurrence without confusion in one personal centre or Self. This justifies indeed the ascription of human predicates to Christ under divine titles, and of divine predicates to Him under human titles. But this is because these titles in any case denote the same central Self of both natures, as distinguished from the particular nature from which His title happens to be taken in the given instance (F. J. Hall, *The Incarnation* [*Dogmatic Theology*, vol. vi, New York:

Longmans, 1915], p. 176 f.; cf. E. L. Mascall, *Christ, the Christian, and the Church* [London: Longmans, 1946], pp. 23-25).

Luther's view, however, assumes a communication of properties or attributes from the divine to the human nature of Christ— hence the doctrine of the ubiquity of Christ's manhood, on which Luther's explanation of the real presence of Christ in the Eucharist is based. This 'divinization' of Christ's humanity is pressed so far that the Lutheran formula can assert that the Word is not outside the flesh (*Logos non extra carnem*) and Lutheran controversialists can stigmatize the *extra Calvinisticum* as a denial of the Incarnation (cf. Bruce, *op. cit.* p. 100). Logically and historically, this supposed fusion of the divine and the human underlies the Kenotic problem. Given other premises, the problem has no meaning. As William Temple says, after setting out the 'intolerable' difficulties of the Kenotic theory:

> All these difficulties are avoided if we suppose that God the Son did indeed most truly live the life recorded in the Gospel, but added this to the other work of God. . . . We are then able to see how Jesus Christ may be truly human, subject to all the conditions of His human life, 'a Jew of the first century', and yet be very God, without any such self-emptying of God as has a mythological appearance and involves stupendous difficulties in general philosophy or theology (*Christus Veritas* [London: Macmillan, 1924], p. 143).

The Lutheran view, however, requires a total identification of human nature with the divine attributes; omnipresence, omniscience, omnipotence, and the rest all belong to the manhood of the Word made flesh. The difficulty of reconciling this idea with the historical reality of Jesus' life aroused conflicts among Lutherans as early as the seventeenth century, when the theologians of Giessen, involved in debate with the more rigidly doctrinaire Lutherans of Tübingen, met the problem by teaching the *kenosis* of the divine attributes *as communicated to Christ's human nature*—a theory which, despite its limited application, did anticipate the Kenoticism of the nineteenth century (cf. K. Barth, *op. cit.* p. 181 f.). It can hardly be claimed that the problem becomes any simpler when Thomasius turns the Lutheran doctrine upside down and, in the interests of a more anthropocentric doctrine of the Incarnation, asserts the communication of human attributes to Christ's deity, since this would appear to safeguard the real humanity of Jesus at the expense of his divine identity. Sound or unsound, however, this adaptation of Lutheran scholasticism is one of the primary sources of modern Kenoticism.

The Christological problem is made still more difficult by the supposition that the unity of Christ's being involves the unity of his 'personality' in the modern popular sense. E. L. Mascall has convincingly shown how this notion bedevilled much of the English Christological thinking of the past half-century or more (*op. cit.* chaps. i-iii). Our immediate concern, however, is simply to note its contribution to Kenotic 'mono-physitism'. The traditional Christology had assumed the possi-bility of speaking of two natures, each with its proper activities, including will and consciousness, without making talk about unity of person completely unintelligible. Once personality was equated with consciousness, this possibility no longer existed; unity of person must involve some kind of suppression of one nature. For the older monophysitism, nourished in a different intellectual and religious setting, it was human nature that seemed in some sense expendable; for the new 'psychological' monophysitism, on the contrary, it was the divine nature that must somehow be adjusted to the indisputable reality of Christ's human life and experience. Here, quite evidently, we have another major doctrinal source of Kenotic speculation.

On such principles as these, the Kenoticists set out to remedy the deficiencies of the Fathers of Chalcedon. The occasional innocent seems to have overlooked the difference between *hypostasis* or *prosopon* and 'person' as currently understood, but most of the Kenotic theorists had a clear idea of the situa-tion. As they saw it, the Fathers may have meant well, but their 'physical' rather than 'ethical' doctrine of personality made it impossible for them to do justice to the living unity of Christ's person—hence the necessity of translating the Catholic doctrine of the Incarnation into new and more adequately 'personal' terms.

> God and man are yoked together, not exhibited in the single-ness of personal life. That this was the preponderating tendency

of Chalcedonian Christology is proved by the Dyophysite and Dyothelite findings of the next three hundred years, and against this tendency Monophysitism offered a valuable protest, so far, by contending that all that is Divine in Christ is human, and all that is human, Divine. Nothing else represents the unity of impression made by the historic Jesus (Mackintosh, *op. cit.* p. 214).

We might readily agree that Monophysitism provided an important reminder of the reality of the divine action in Christ, over against the Nestorian dissolution of the ultimate unity of the divine-human work of redemption. But what Nestorius seems to have been trying to say—even if in a bumbling and not too perceptive way—was, as he himself was to claim, at least one of the important things that Chalcedon said. Ever since Chalcedon canonized the genuine truth of the Antiochene Christology, it has been clear that the Christology of the Catholic Church—over against all 'monophysitisms', past, present, and future—stands for the union of the Logos with a concrete human nature, physically and psychically complete, formed of individual soul and body. The union, it is true, needs careful and emphatic expression to safeguard its uniqueness, but— at least as the traditional Christology sees it—it is an ontological rather than a psychological union, or, in Chalcedonian terms, a union in *person*, not in *nature*. It is at least conceivable, surely, that the Fathers did not merely stumble into this distinction but, on the contrary, adopted it deliberately as the surest defence of Christian faith in the God-Man. At all events, they did build a Christological structure within which, because of the distinction of natures, there is as much room as in any Kenotic system for the recognition of the human reality of Jesus' temporal existence.

The Kenotic theologians, nevertheless, are profoundly dissatisfied with this doctrine because, to their minds, it does not allow for a real Incarnation. It does not present the one Lord Jesus Christ, God and man, as a psychological unity; it does not make room for the utter self-abnegation of God in becoming man. We must ask, however, whether any ultimately defensible doctrine of the Incarnation could conceivably meet these Kenotic requirements. Certainly the traditional Christology declines to try to meet them, on the ground of the principle of divine immutability, and as long as that principle stands there can be no place for a Kenotic doctrine in Christian thought. The Kenoticists, however, are convinced that the concept of immutability requires radical revision in the light of the Christian revelation of God's love. 'Sheer unchangeableness', says Mackintosh, 'is, of course, something against which no human pleading can bear up; but it is worth asking whether it ought to figure in a Christian argument' (*op. cit.* p. 472 f.).

It would be unfair to ascribe to Kenoticism as a whole those theories which have justly been described as 'crudely external in their treatment of the divine attributes' (L. S. Thornton, C.R., *The Incarnate Lord* [London: Longmans, 1928], p. 262), since few if any theologians would now want to defend the treatment of the attributes of deity as so many articles of clothing, to be put on or taken off at will. But it is not unreasonable to ask whether the more sophisticated doctrine of Forsyth and Mackintosh—and, apparently, of Vincent Taylor (cf. *The Person of Christ in New Testament Teaching* [London: Macmillan, 1958], p. 293 f.)—is really any better. Forsyth puts the newer doctrine plainly:

> The kenotic process . . . does not think of the divine self-consciousness as going out of existence, but only of its retraction, concentration, or occultation, in one constituent of the Godhead. The suicide of God is no part of the kenotic idea, which turns but on self-divestment as a moral power of the eternal Son; who retains his consciousness but renounces the conditions of infinity and its precreate form (*The Person and Place of Jesus Christ* [London: Independent Press, 1951], p. 295 f.).

And a little later he writes: 'We have not so much the renunciation of attributes, nor their conscious possession and concealment, as the retraction of their mode of being from actual to potential' (*ibid.* p. 308; cf. Mackintosh, *op. cit.* p. 477). Just what are we to make of this revised version of Kenoticism?

While less 'crudely external' than the original theory, it still presents serious difficulties from the standpoint of traditional Christian theism. The notion of the 'retraction' of the divine attributes from 'full actuality' to 'concentrated potency' (Mackintosh, *loc. cit.*) implies both a real ontological change in

God and a still somewhat external and mechanical idea of the relation of God's attributes to his being as God, and these ascriptions of mutation and composition to God run counter to the eternal changelessness and the perfect simplicity of infinite and transcendent Spirit, in which Christian theology has commonly found the very meaning of deity. Our authors, it is true, deal quite summarily with this kind of difficulty, by drawing a sharp contrast between the 'metaphysical' and the 'ethical'—or at least between a metaphysic whose categories are 'physical and partially mechanical' and a 'metaphysic of the conscience, in which not substance but Holy Love is supreme' (Mackintosh, *op. cit.* p. 472). So, for instance, Mackintosh writes: 'If the alternatives are an unethical conception of immutability and a pure thought of moral omnipotence, which makes room for Divine sacrifice, the Christian mind need not hesitate' (*ibid.* p. 474). A. M. Fairbairn expresses the same idea, in the context of a developed philosophy of deity:

> Whatever . . . could be surrendered, the ethical attributes and qualities could not; but God may only seem the more Godlike if, in obedience to the ethical, He limit or restrain or veil the physical. . . . So conceived, then, the Incarnation may be described as the most illustrious example of the supremacy of God's moral over His physical attributes, and of the relation they hold to the healing and the happiness of man (*The Place of Christ in Modern Theology* [2nd ed., London: Hodder and Stoughton, 1893], p. 476 f.).

Forsyth states the underlying principle abruptly: 'God is God not physically but morally, not by power but by love. That is the Christian revelation' (*op. cit.* p. 313). Some of us, however, may find it difficult to identify the Christian revelation quite so completely with a voluntaristic philosophy of religion, whether Ockhamist or Kantian, especially when we recall that such a philosophy, with its exaltation of will over being and reason, has helped to produce some of the worst theological monstrosities in Christian history—the rigid Calvinist doctrine of predestination being only one peculiarly ominous example. On the contrary, even at the cost of excluding Kenotic views of what the Incarnation ought to involve, we may find ourselves compelled by the witness both of Scripture and of reason to God's eternal power and divinity to say with Karl Barth:

> God is always God even in His humiliation. The divine being does not suffer any change, any diminution, any transformation into something else, any admixture with something else, let alone any cessation. The deity of Christ is the one unaltered because unalterable deity of God. Any subtraction or weakening of it would at once throw doubt upon the atonement made in Him. He humbled Himself, but He did not do it by ceasing to be who He is (*op. cit.* p. 179 f.).

Barth's insistence on the unaltered deity of Christ as the presupposition of his atoning work takes us the last step of the way. It is often urged in defence of Kenotic ideas of what the Incarnation must mean that they alone ensure the 'religious' significance of Christian doctrine. Barth, on the contrary, regards such ideas as destructive of the Gospel of redemption, and therefore, presumably, of what the Kenoticists themselves would see as the heart of the Christian 'religion'. But perhaps we need to press the question a little further, and ask what rights 'religion' can have against truth. It can hardly be claimed that Kenoticism is explicitly contained in the New Testament picture of Christ; rather, it depends on a complicated deduction, involving highly debatable presuppositions. Nor can it be said that Kenoticism lacks serious difficulties, inherent in its flat contradiction of the traditional Christian understanding of the divine nature. Of course, if the Kenotic theory could prove its case against traditional theism, these difficulties would evaporate. But as long as that case remains unproved—and we have seen no reason to regard it as already demonstrated—no appeal to 'religion' can justify an evasion of insuperable intellectual obstacles. For it is of the essence of the Christian religion, over against those false worships whose cruel idolatries Lucretius summed up for all time in his pregnant saying, *Tantum religio potuit suadere malorum*, to be a communion in spirit and truth with the one true God. It follows, if we accept the judgment of Christian history on the theological principle of Kenoticism, that the Kenotic theory does not in fact vindicate the religious meaning of the Christian Gospel. On the contrary, in the severe words of Pius XII, it 'turns the integral mystery of the Incarnation and of redemption into bloodless and empty spectres' (Encyclical, *Sempiternus Rex Christus* [*A.A.S.*, 43 (1951), p. 638]). Or, as Ritschl says more bluntly still: 'This way of confessing Christ's Godhead is a ceremony that has lost its meaning' (*The Christian Doctrine of Justification and Reconciliation* [Edinburgh: T. & T. Clark, 1900], p. 411).

INDEXES

I. INDEX OF BIBLICAL REFERENCES

INDEX OF BIBLICAL REFERENCES

II. INDEX OF GREEK WORDS

Note: Words given only in transliteration are put in parentheses.

III. GENERAL INDEX

Date Due